Twenty Years in South Africa

Twenty Years in South Africa

•An Immigrant's Tale•

MICHAEL J. LOWIS

Foreword by Roger Kendall

RESOURCE *Publications* • Eugene, Oregon

TWENTY YEARS IN SOUTH AFRICA
An Immigrant's Tale

Copyright © 2017 Michael J. Lowis. All rights reserved. Except for brief quotations in critical publications or reviews, no part of this book may be reproduced in any manner without prior written permission from the publisher. Write: Permissions, Wipf and Stock Publishers, 199 W. 8th Ave., Suite 3, Eugene, OR 97401.

Resource Publications
An Imprint of Wipf and Stock Publishers
199 W. 8th Ave., Suite 3
Eugene, OR 97401

www.wipfandstock.com

PAPERBACK ISBN: 978-1-5326-1777-5
HARDCOVER ISBN: 978-1-4982-4272-1
EBOOK ISBN: 978-1-4982-4271-4

Manufactured in the U.S.A.					FEBRUARY 28, 2017

Contents

List of Illustrations | vi
Foreword by Roger Kendall | vii
Preface | ix
Acknowledgements | xi

Chapter 1	Why South Africa?	1
Chapter 2	The Journey	5
Chapter 3	The Arrival	12
Chapter 4	Getting Down to Business	19
Chapter 5	The Music	27
Chapter 6	Rhodesia and Lesotho	35
Chapter 7	Taking Stock	41
Chapter 8	Swaziland, Swa, and Botswana	49
Chapter 9	The Animals	56
Chapter 10	The Places	63
Chapter 11	Further Reflections	70
Chapter 12	The Law, Guns, and Danger	78
Chapter 13	Work and Play	86
Chapter 14	Customs and Culture	94
Chapter 15	The Food	102
Chapter 16	Diversion	108
Chapter 17	The First Democratic Elections	113
Chapter 18	Life after the Election	122

Afterword: Was It Worth It? | 131

List of Illustrations

Figure 1. The ballot paper for the first democratic elections | 119

Foreword

IN A PUBLISHING WORLD dominated by the autobiographies and memoirs of politicians and celebrities, how refreshing it is to glimpse the day-to-day lives of ordinary people. Of course Mike Lowis's decision to find employment in South Africa and move his young family there was no ordinary adventure, and his memoir is a fascinating read for this reason alone.

I was privileged to follow Mike's journey chapter by chapter, so for me the whole enterprise unfolded in stages, much as it did for the Lowis family. From the voyage out (an assisted passage) to the first sight of land and the description of the dawn breaking over Table Mountain, we are "put in the picture" by Mike's vivid descriptions of the South African landscape.

Especially enjoyable are Mike's amusing descriptions of their encounters with South African bureaucracy and officialdom; in fact, humor runs through his narrative, and we are introduced to many off-beat characters and situations along the way. As the family settles in to their new home and finds their feet, one is reminded of Gerald Durrell's memoir of his years in Corfu in *My Family and Other Animals,* and of particular interest to me as a WWF member was the Lowis family's wildlife safari and the animals they spotted in the national park and elsewhere.

But this memoir is about so much more than South Africa's 'Big Game.' The Lowis family's stay coincided with the last years of

Foreword

Apartheid, Nelson Mandela's release and the first democratic elections. Not knowing much about South African history, or the political, economic and social situation when I began reading these memoirs, I was truly indebted to Mike Lowis for sketching in the background to his family's 20-year sojourn.

One of the great strengths of this memoir is that Mike Lowis is able to include the perspectives of his wife and three boys—to school, to growing up in a strange new country, to home life, including dog walking—in fact, the life, as it's lived by many present-day South African families.

Mike also broadens his narrative with chapters on South African culture, music and singing, traditional food (I now know what "Bunny Chow" and "Fat Cooks" are!), and the traditions and social relations of both black and white, so that the reader feels, as the account draws to a close and the family return to England, that one has been informed with a greater understanding of this varied and multi-faceted country.

Roger Kendall
Ripon
United Kingdom
December, 2016

Preface

WAS IT FOOLHARDY FOR a British family to make the decision to emigrate to South Africa during the height of the apartheid era? This was the year 1975. The decision to leave Britain was motivated as much by the desire to escape from the poor weather and economic stagnation, as it was to experience a different way of life in a new country. What was originally intended as an extended holiday of just a year or two, before then returning to the grind, turned out to be almost 20 years.

During the stay in our adopted country, we visited all the major towns and game parks, and some of the neighboring countries. We certainly did see many fascinating things, and met many wonderful people. There were countless high points, but also some low ones that could have had life-changing consequences. The earlier years belonged to a time of oppression of the majority by minority, which came to a head with the Soweto riots in 1976. The death toll from this event shocked South Africans, and those in many other countries of the world.

Gradually, signs of change started to appear and, in 1990, Nelson Mandela was released from prison. The long and painful journey to democratization was completed with the first fully-inclusive elections in 1994. Before we returned to the UK in 1995, we were able to see first-hand the start of the effects that majority rule had on the lives of all population groups. Since that time, we

Preface

have kept in touch with many of the friends we made during stay in South Africa, and have received regular updates on the social and political developments there.

Drawing on an archive of tape recordings and photographs to reinforce our memories, this narrative is an attempt to help readers share our observations and experiences—both good and bad—of living in South Africa during those eventful times. The situation in the country we called home for 20 years has changed significantly since our stay there. This account is, therefore, a record of times now past. In addition to it providing a few hours of diversion for the general reader, it should have additional value as a resource for those interested in the social history of that nation at that time.

Michael J. Lowis
Northampton
United Kingdom
January, 2017

Acknowledgements

It would be rare for any book to be the work of just one person. My wife, Susan, has specifically contributed to two of the chapters in addition to jogging my memory when necessary. Our sons Peter, David, and Charles have all shared snippets of information here and there, which have helped to add those little extra details. For this family help, I am very grateful.

We left South Africa and returned to the UK a year after the first democratic elections in 1995. In order to include an update on the developments since that time, I am indebted to several friends who still live in the country we called home for 20 years. They have been kind enough to provide valuable opinion and details of the current situation, these supplement the reports that have appeared in the news media from time to time.

It would be impossible to mention individually the many lovely people of all races who welcomed us when we arrived, and who helped us during our stay in their wonderful country. We could have been resented and rejected, but we ended up making many friends, some with whom we remain in contact to this day. Thank you all you dear people, for providing me with the many experiences that have inspired this book.

Finally, many thanks to Dr Roger Kendall, Member of The Society of Authors and Course Tutor for *Writing Magazine*. Not only did he readily agree to write the foreword for this book, but

Acknowledgements

he also suggested revisions and grammatical corrections that have proved invaluable in the preparation of the final manuscript.

Chapter 1

Why South Africa?

THE YEAR WAS 1975; the place was the Yorkshire town of Halifax, in the United Kingdom. Why would anyone want to leave a safe, democratic country that has a National Health Service, freedom of speech, and no policy of racial discrimination, for one in the throes of apartheid, draconian laws, violence, and with no social welfare? But was the UK in the early 1970s indeed a utopia from which it would have been foolhardy to leave?

Although I had a steady, managerial job in the food manufacturing industry, there seemed to be little chance for promotion within the foreseeable future. The British economy was in a period of recession, there was double-digit inflation and strikes were frequent—especially by the coal miners. Much of industry was forced to work a Three-Day Week, due to power shortages.

This restriction was particularly critical for the factory where I worked. Food was baked on metal conveyor belts that passed through long, electrically heated ovens. These required time to heat up, and to cool down, in addition to the period when they were actually doing the baking. If the belts stopped suddenly, for example due to a power failure, the food already inside the oven would catch fire. This could then spread. Thus, once powered-up, the ovens often ran for days around the clock. Equipment like this standing idle resulted in significant financial losses for the company.

It was time for me to think hard about my career, and the quality of life that my wife and young family deserved. Surely there should be something better than this. But where to find it? Emigration appeared to be the only option. When we were first married, my wife Susan and I applied for emigration to Australia under the assisted passage scheme. At the time, there was a flat charge of 10 British pounds for each person, for door-to-door transport to that country. We were young, and the prospect seemed exciting. Before taking the plunge, however, it seemed a good idea to first secure a specific job, and to know exactly where it would be. This had not been successful by the time it was necessary to accept or reject the offer of a specific flight and departure date. Somewhat reluctantly, we declined this opportunity, although later we sometimes wondered if it had been the right decision.

About 10 years later, and now with two young sons, I suggested to Susan that we might want to think again about emigrating. This came as somewhat of a surprise to her. After some consideration, Susan's response was, "Well, I suppose going to some interesting country and seeing the world for two or three years would be a good experience for all of us." Following a short pause, she then asked, "But where would be a suitable place to go?"

Many thoughts flooded into our minds. What would our children think? What would our own parents make of this? Could we afford it? Would there be suitable employment for me?

The choice of country was underpinned by several important criteria. Firstly, it should be a place where English was spoken and, secondly, there should be a growing economy where technical and managerial skills were in demand. It should also be a country that had both an available labor force, and a good supply of natural resources. In the UK at that time, many raw materials had to be imported, which sometimes led to shortages and spiraling costs. Despite the recession, it was difficult to recruit workers for the more menial jobs, and machines then stood idle for lack of operators. Our final consideration was that it would be nice to have a decent, temperate climate where our children could enjoy a healthy upbringing. Eventually, a short-list emerged: Australia,

Canada, the USA, the West Indies, and South Africa. After much investigation and deliberation, our choice was the latter.

Apart from ticking all these boxes, a big incentive in favor of South Africa was the assisted passage scheme that existed at the time. This meant that it would cost us very little money to make the long journey to that country. The government there needed to encourage an influx of people with appropriate education and skills, especially to help develop and manage the manufacturing industry. Whilst this was a significant "plus", there was also a big "minus": the political situation. The South Africa government was enforcing a policy of "apartheid"—an Afrikaans word meaning "separate development". Taken literally, this may not have seemed to be too problematic. As we were eventually to experience for ourselves, in reality, it manifested itself as *unequal* development.

Once we were committed to going to live on the Southern African continent, there was no looking back. The planning and organizing of our emigration took a full year. There were many formalities to complete, starting with our application to the South African embassy in London. We were interviewed by an immigration official, and detailed medical examinations were carried out on each of us. Vaccination certificates were issued to ensure we had been protected against smallpox.

As the main bread winner, it was necessary for me to be classified as employable. Rather than just leave it to the authorities to find me a job, it seemed to be a good idea for me to send my curriculum vitae to several South African food manufacturing companies, and ask if they had any suitable vacancies. A few of them did reply, including one in the Johannesburg area that asked me to contact them for an interview as soon as we arrived. Such a positive response helped to dispel any doubts about the wisdom of our decision to emigrate. However, my wife's comment about going away for "two or three years" was to prove to be quite an underestimate!

In due course, we were supplied with our entry permits. Had we chosen to travel by air, the whole journey would have been free. Instead we decided that it would add to our adventure if we travelled by sea, even though this would incur an additional cost. In those days the *Union Castle* mail ships were still operating between England and South Africa, and our passage was booked on the *Pendennis Castle*. This vessel weighed just over 28,000 tons and carried 670 passengers, most of whom, we were later to discover, seemed to be fellow immigrants.

We were fortunate that we managed to sell our house in Halifax, UK, but were able to remain there until the day of our departure. It was not easy parting with all our furnishings and possessions, apart from what could be accommodated in six, sturdy cardboard boxes that would be sent off ahead of us. If this was hard, then our farewell round of visits to friends and relatives was even more so.

A common reaction was, "Why on earth do you want to go to that violent and undemocratic country?" Whilst good reasons could be given to counter this, another question was much more difficult to answer. Our parents in particular asked, "How can I see my grandchildren growing up when you will be living thousands of miles away?" Most painful of all was, "How can you emigrate at this time when a close relative is seriously ill?"

Ethical dilemmas such as those posed in the last two questions cannot be answered by reasoning alone, and they continue to haunt over 40 years later. Were we justified in following what could be regarded as a selfish pursuit of the good life, whilst being inconsiderate of what others may think? Should we cancel a year's preparation at this late stage? There was a time limit on our immigration permits. If we postponed our trip now, could we resurrect it later?

Rightly or wrongly, after much soul-searching, we put the future of our nuclear family first, and continued with our planned emigration. It was, however, with a very heavy heart, and more than a few tears, that we made our final visits to people we might never see again. How do we feel about this decision now? We have asked ourselves this question many times over the years. Certainly we were to have our ups and downs, failures and successes, but was it worth it? We shall return to this question in due course.

Chapter 2

The Journey

IT WAS STILL DARK as our ship entered the docks at Cape Town, so the famous Table Mountain that we had travelled 6,000 miles to see was completely invisible. Much had happened to us over the last two weeks, but soon we would be starting a new life that, up to now, we could only imagine. Despite now being on the cusp of the unknown, we remained excited about what was in store for us. Our previous life in England seemed a long way away.

One of my last actions before we left home was to buy a portable cassette audio recorder. Back in the 1970s they were the new technology and relatively expensive. We were embarking on the adventure of a lifetime, and there would no doubt be opportunities to record some of our thoughts and feelings along the way. Also, rather than just writing letters to the folks back home, we thought it would be nice to send them audio tapes as well. Now, some 40 years later, several of these recorded narratives still exist, and are being drawn on as aides-memoire for this book. The earliest tape certainly brings back memories, as it contains a brief daily log of our boat journey from Southampton to Cape Town—a distance of about 6,000 nautical miles—which took 12 days.

We had not been on a large, ocean-going vessel before, and the *Pendennis Castle* looked enormous, despite being significantly smaller than most cruise liners are today. With mixed feelings of excitement, sadness, and trepidation we boarded the ship, after having spent the previous night in a hotel near the port. We were shown to the two adjacent outside cabins that would be home respectively to Susan and me, and our children—Peter, who was then aged nine, and David who was six—for nearly two weeks. This was a two-class ship, and of course we were in the lower one. The accommodation had a pair of bunk beds, a dressing table, and some storage space, but no bathroom; the communal ablutions were a short distance away. Once again, with our lack of prior experience, we did not appreciate the relative Spartan quality of these cabins when compared with even the most basic ones on cruise liners today.

Our feelings of adventure grew ever stronger as the time for departure approached. Eventually, the last gangway was hoisted on board, and the ship pulled slowly away from the quayside. Many people were there to wave off their friends and relatives, although sadly there was nobody there for us. Perhaps this was just as well, because the emotion of leaving behind loved ones, some of whom we would not see again, might have been just too much to bear. As Southampton gradually receded into the distance, we took the customary photographs of us on deck, and what would be our last glimpse of England in the background. Viewing them again now, Peter and David look excited; Susan seems pensive and a little sad; my expression shows me wondering just what will be in store for us in the days, weeks, months and even years to come.

We then turned away from the country of our birth—turned away from the thought of it, as well as the sight—and went below to prepare for the obligatory emergency drill that would begin in 30 minutes time.

It took a day or two for us not to feel any sea-sickness, and our youngest son had to have some treatment for it from the medical staff. Poor David, although he seemed to be excited by the adventure, he was also probably anxious about the future, and this could well have exacerbated his sickness. Eventually, however, we all became acclimatized to the motion of the ship, ready to enjoy the trip and join in the fun and games.

The Journey

For Susan and me, the first highlight of the voyage came on the third day: the captain's cocktail party. The children were able to eat before the adults, and were then supervised so that their parents could dine without having to worry about them. Thus, free from parental responsibilities, that evening we dressed in our finest clothes and joined the queue to be introduced to our Captain. He shook hands with everyone. We were graciously welcomed, and then pointed in the direction of staff who were holding trays of drinks and canapés. The officers had been given permission to change from their blue uniforms to white tropical outfits, and they were obviously very pleased to be able to do this and feel more relaxed. My! But we felt important, hobnobbing with the great and the good—a new experience for us. The audio log has me exclaiming, "We started to feel we were really living it up!"

During the late afternoon of the fourth day, we had our only landfall of the journey. The first sight of the island of Gran Canaria was a small pimple on the horizon, and we then watched with fascination as it grew steadily closer so that some features could be recognized. We sailed into the port of Las Palmas as the light was fading, and tied up at the quayside side. The ship's crew immediately started to busy themselves taking on water, fuel and food supplies. Because it would shortly be dark, the only tourist option was to take an organized bus tour of some of the main sites around the town. The most notable memory of this trip was being taken high up on a hill, and looking down on the twinkling lights of the town and the harbor. We could just make out our ship, looking surprisingly small and vulnerable at that distance. Back on board, and weary after a long day, we were glad to tumble into our bunks and were soon in the land of dreams.

Now feeling quite well and relaxed, over the next few days we enjoyed taking part in the usual deck games, entering the competitions, watching the entertainment and, perhaps most of all, eating all the lovely food—without having to do the washing up! We had not often been able to afford to visit restaurants in the UK, but now we were dining out every day. We also joined a tour to the ship's bridge. This control centre of the ship turned out to be a very relaxed place in mid-voyage. The little activity that there was comprised periodic scrutiny of the horizon through binoculars by a duty officer. In addition to the BBC radio news being relayed over the public address system at 12 noon, each day we were issued with a small newspaper called the *Ocean Mail*. This included world news items, sports results, the weather, and shipboard announcements. We were thus kept well informed of current events.

The closest approach to land during the voyage, apart from the stop at Las Palmas, was when we rounded the bulge of the west coast of Africa. The Cape Verde Islands were to the west of us, and Senegal to the east. We were told that, on a clear day, you could make out some of the buildings of the capital, Dakar, on the mainland. However, apart from what may have been a brief glimpse through the haze of something square-shaped, we saw nothing. What we did notice, now that we were fairly close to land on both sides, were birds flying near the ship. Until then, it had not struck us that they had been absent. Were the flocks migrating, we wondered, or just coming to say "Hello"? Looking down into the ocean we saw flying fish skimming the water for surprisingly long distances.

A very noteworthy event occurred on the seventh day—crossing the equator. One of my previous work colleagues had on his office wall a certificate that confirmed he had participated in the traditional ritual; I had always longed for one of these documents for myself. The fun and games started at ten-thirty in the morning. The swimming pool was dyed green, and crew members were suitably disguised as King Neptune and his wife, and the demon barber. These and other people then acted out a comical pantomime of mock trials, which always ended in a guilty verdict. The punishment was of being lathered by the barber and then tipped off the chair into the water. After this, the children lined up and paraded around the pool, said "Hello" to the king, and received a dab of foam from the barber.

Once all this was over, each child received a copy of the appropriate certificate from the purser. When I asked if it would be possible to have one of these for myself, he replied that they were only intended for the children who had taken part. "Oh dear", I said. "It has long been one of my ambitions to have such a document. Is there anything you can do?" The purser promised to look into this, and he later reported back that one would be given to me, but only when the voyage was over so as not to prompt others to make the same request. Although now pacified, perhaps it had been a bit foolish, and selfish, to ask for a concession that would not be made to all the other adults on board. Ah well, rightly or wrongly, the certificate confirming my "crossing of the line" now graces my own wall.

One might have imagined that the weather on the equator would be hot and sunny, but my log confirms that instead it was mild, cloudy, and breezy. In fact, we had yet to experience anything resembling tropical conditions since we left England. Just past the half-way point of our voyage, an announcement was made over the public address system. It told us that we would shortly be passing another of the Union Castle mail ships that was heading back to the UK. It was the *Windsor Castle*, and each vessel sounded loud blasts on their whistles whilst passengers lined the decks and waved to each other. This was also the time when we were requested to stop using British currency on board, and start paying with South African rands. The purser was able to exchange our British pounds, and we had our first look at what we rather unkindly called "Mickey Mouse Money".

Over the next day or two we had several very informative documentaries and presentations about the country in which we would soon be living. This was an excellent service for ship's passengers comprising mostly of immigrants, and it helped to prepare us for some of the customs and procedures we would encounter. There was even some entertainment by crew members who were probably South Africans, including a comedian. We learned that the most common family name among Afrikaans white nationals was Van der Merwe but, rather incongruously perhaps, a character of this name was often the "butt" of jokes. Most countries have a "fall guy" for their jokes, but this was like using "Smith" in British humor. What it did indicate, however, was the admirable ability to laugh at oneself.

We were also told that there is a saying among the locals that sums up all that is praiseworthy about South Africa: "Sunny skies, braaivleis and rugby!" Although "braaivleis" is Afrikaans for "barbeque", this word is used universally in the country, and is often abbreviated to "braai".

As our destination grew ever closer, we could often feel the ship swaying due to the Cape Rollers, large waves that sweep across the Atlantic Ocean unimpeded until they hit the western shores of Southern Africa. The last notable event on board was a fancy dress competition for both adults and children. Some passengers were clearly anticipating this, as they had either brought some appropriate props with them, or had been cleverly fabricating them whilst on board. Although the on-board shops did sell materials, we wanted to save our limited funds. Instead we had the idea of using some very large paper towels that were available, as playing cards. When we tied two of them end to end, and used red lipstick to paint a large ace of hearts on one pair, and an ace of diamonds on the other, we could slip them over the heads of our boys like sandwich boards, and announce them as "The Two Aces".

Susan and I did not dress up, but at least Peter and David joined the parade, and a good time was had by all. One slim passenger had managed to paint a skeleton on a garment that covered most of his body. He carried a placard that stated: "Eat well on the *Pendennis Castle*" This caused much laughter, but resulted in a rather pained expression from the purser who was introducing everybody. One other character that we still remember was a rather tubby lady dressed as a fairy, and with a label that read: "Sugar Plump Fairy!" By an amazing coincidence, we were to meet this person again about 18 months later, along with another family who, unbeknown to us at the time, had also been on this same ship.

It was our last night on board. Our bags were packed, and we had received all the necessary information for disembarking the next day. We would soon be leaving this vessel that we had come to know so well, a ship that had fed us, entertained us, and transported us half way round the world. The holiday was over, and the serious task of establishing a new life would now begin. We were very glad that we had chosen to come by sea, so that we could gradually prepare ourselves for this change. How much more difficult it would have been to do this had we made the journey by air in just 12 hours instead of 12 days. Our estimated arrival time in Cape Town would be five-thirty the following morning. What would we see? What would we experience? Would there be any unforeseen problems? We would surely find out soon enough.

Chapter 3

The Arrival

THE DATE WAS THE fifth of November, 1975; the time was five-thirty in the morning. The ship was still, the engines were silent; our 12-day journey must be over. Hooray! A quick look through the porthole: only blackness. We must have anchored in Table Bay, and the temptation to go on deck and see the iconic Table Mountain first hand was irresistible. It would be wonderful to be able to capture on film the first rays of sun hitting this titanic square of rock. Once outside, a few stars were still visible. Looking across to the land, all that could be seen were the distant lights of the city stretching to the right and the left, and rising gently backwards. Between where the lights stopped and the stars in the sky began there was a slab of total blackness. How very puzzling—was this an optical illusion? In the darkness, there was no obvious explanation. Could there be a gigantic mass of something out there, blocking the view? It is perhaps surprising that it took time for the reality to sink in—this just had to be Table Mountain.

The minutes seemed to take hours, but then to the west there was the first glimmer of light to indicate that dawn was breaking. Very gradually, the magnificent mountain came into view, and it was a truly breathtaking sight. There was this great flat-topped natural wonder right in front of me, the grayish granite of its sheer slopes reflecting back the early sunlight. Like sentinels on guard, it was flanked on the left by an outcrop called the Devil's Peak, and by the pointed top of the Lion's Head hill on the right. The spectacle did not disappoint. My travels over the years have allowed me to see a number of the world's most spectacular sights but, when people ask me which was the most awe inspiring, the answer is always what was transfixing my gaze at that moment. Any attempts to preserve the experience on film do not do justice to this vision as seen with the naked eye.

Eventually it was time to drag myself away and join the family for our last breakfast on board. There were many formalities to complete before we could disembark, starting with a vaccination check by a health officer. At about mid-day we left the ship, and identified the six cardboard boxes of all that remained of the home we had back in England. During the voyage, these had been stored in the ship's hold. These and our other luggage were checked by a customs man whose main concern was whether or not we were importing a television receiver. On assuring him that we were not, he issued us with the necessary paperwork to leave the port.

Curious to know why televisions were apparently so important, we learned that South Africa was one of the very few developed countries of the world not to have a fully-established TV network at that time. There had been an outcry amongst the population when, in 1969, the Americans first landed on the Moon. South Africa was unique among the civilized nations in not being able to relay this event live. Some people said that television had not been introduced for political reasons, and that the government did not want the general population to see how the rest of the world lived. This seemed to be a rather cynical view, and we never found out if it was indeed correct.

Notwithstanding this, a limited television service was currently being introduced, but the receivers were still relatively expensive. There was a law that one could not buy a set without first obtaining a license and showing it to the shopkeeper. Hence, had we been secretly importing a television with our luggage, we would have been able to escape the license fee, should we have been so inclined.

The next formality was with the immigration authorities. Our documentation was checked and found to be in order, so we were now officially "permanent residents" of South Africa. We said that we now needed to travel to Johannesburg, and were duly issued with vouchers for the "Trans-Karoo Express" train leaving the next day. Arrangements were made for our six cardboard boxes of possessions to be transported separately by freight train, so that we could collect them from the railway depot at Johannesburg. The officer then gave each of us a label to pin on our clothing when we arrived at our destination, to show that we were immigrants. An official would meet us at the station there to escort us to an immigration hotel. Oh dear! Labels pinned to our clothes? We would feel like refugee children did in the last war, or perhaps Paddington Bear arriving from "Darkest Peru", as depicted by author Michael Bond.

Eventually we were free to await transport to the accommodation that had been pre-booked whilst we were still on the *Pendennis Castle*. After a short taxi drive to the Skyway Hotel, and hungry after a long morning, we unloaded our cases and set off to find a place for lunch. The food was enjoyable and inexpensive, the sky was blue and the sun was shining; we had arrived in one piece; we felt good. As we only had the rest of that day to explore Cape Town, what should we do? Firstly, we took a bus to Camps Bay, a beach to the east of the main town. This was an idyllic spot, with the golden sand and azure ocean in front of us, and the spectacular mountain peaks of the Twelve Apostles at our backs. The sea was inviting, so we paddled in with our bare feet—and it was freezing! We did not realize that the cold Atlantic current laps the shores of Cape Town, and that it was necessary to go further around the coast to the east to catch the warm Indian Ocean.

It was now mid-afternoon, and we decided that the opportunity to take the cable car to the top of Table Mountain should not be wasted. There was some initial reluctance among the family members for doing this, because the prospect of making this steep ascent in what looked like a fragile little box was a bit frightening. Nevertheless, we took a taxi to the lower cable station and, as the gondola ascended, we tried not to think about the long drop beneath us. The top of the mountain was composed of rocks and boulders of all sizes, interspersed with green bushes. Pathways had been trodden by countless numbers of hikers, and there was even a stone building set well back from the edge. Needless to say, the view over the city and out to sea in this clear air was absolutely stunning. The ships in the harbor looked as small as ants and, out in the bay, we could see Robben Island, with its notorious prison which, at that time in 1975, was home to Nelson Mandela and other political prisoners.

It had been a long day, but we felt that we had made the most of our very short stay in this beautiful city. We descended the mountain and returned to our hotel to freshen ourselves up ready for the evening meal. Fate, however, still had something up its sleeve for me: I became stuck in the bathroom! Despite all efforts to open it, the lock on the door had jammed. My wife had to telephone for the hotel manager to come up and release me. After trying unsuccessfully to open the door from the outside, he had no alternative but to use brute force. Eventually I was free from my temporary jail, albeit it a bit embarrassed when confronted by the manager. We have laughed about this since, and can never resist breaking into the "unofficial" words of a well-known nursery rhyme: "Oh dear, what can the matter be, two old ladies locked in the lavatory!"

The next morning we made our way to the railway station and boarded the Trans-Karoo Express that would take us to Johannesburg. We were very pleased to find that our family had been booked into our very own compartment, which easily accommodated the four of us. There were bunk beds that could be unfolded from the walls, a table, and even a wash basin set against the outside window. The holiday feeling remained with us, although we were fully aware that the reality of trying to establish a new life in our adopted country would soon catch up with us. Still, we thought, why not enjoy it whilst we can. We had been allocated our meal times in the restaurant car, and could have no complaints about the quality of the food we were served there.

The train passed through a great variety of terrain during its nearly 1,000-mile journey. Firstly, there was a continuation of the sort of impressive mountain scenery that we had seen in Cape Town, and even some flat-topped peaks that looked like cousins of Table Mountain itself. After a few hours, the train reached the fringes of the Great Karoo—a semi desert region of 153,000 square miles—and stopped at the little town of Matjiesfontein. Right outside the window was the old colonial Lord Milner Hotel, its notched parapet on the roof giving it the look of a small castle. This building was completed in 1899, and was named after Lord Alfred Milner who was governor of the Cape during the Anglo-Boer War.

A mile or two later, the train commenced its transit of the Karoo. Short, hardy shrubs peppered the landscape, and we could see a few dusty tracks criss-crossing this arid region. Although the guidebooks stated that there was some wildlife there, plus sheep being raised on scattered farms, we did not see any living creature during this part of the journey. We were to learn later that the Karoo does in fact receive some rainfall, and that underground water can be tapped by boreholes. The afternoon was drawing to a close, and the light was fading. Still feeling the proverbial tourist, there was an opportunity for one final photograph—of the red sunset over the desert.

During the night, the train completed its traverse of the Great Karoo and gradually climbed up to an elevation of 4,000 feet, where it stopped at the "Diamond City" of Kimberley. Because the line northwards had been electrified, it was necessary to replace the diesel-powered engine with an electric locomotive. Even had it been daylight, the station was unfortunately too far away from the world's biggest man-made hole—an open-cast diamond mine—for us to have been able to see anything of it on this occasion. Tomorrow, after climbing still higher to an altitude of 6,000 feet, we would arrive at Johannesburg, and the serious business of establishing ourselves in our adopted land would begin.

As the train pulled into the station, we peered out of the window and glimpsed some of the tall, white buildings of this, South Africa's largest, city. After we had pinned on our rather

The Arrival

embarrassing immigrant identity labels, we alighted and unloaded our hand luggage onto the platform. Almost immediately, we were located by the official who had been sent to meet us. He gave us a friendly welcome, and explained that he would take us to one of the hotels allocated to immigrants. We would initially be able to stay there free for up to two weeks, depending on how quickly we could find a job and somewhere of our own to live. This all seemed to be very well organized and generous. Finally, the official gave us several pages of instructions about what to do next, starting with a visit to the immigration office first thing on Monday morning.

The hotel was in Edith Cavell Street, near the Hillbrow district of the city. Whilst not exactly luxury accommodation, it was certainly adequate and we could have no complaints. One abiding memory of our stay there was that just about every meal except breakfast served overcooked gem squash. For the uninitiated, this vegetable is round, dark green, and a bit larger than an apple. It is boiled, and then cut in half, and it tastes somewhat like a pumpkin. So satiated did we become with this "delicacy", that it was a long time before we could bring ourselves to cook this vegetable in our own home.

By a happy coincidence, the next day was a Sunday, so we still had one day left before getting down to business. It would be a good opportunity to explore the city. Prior to 1886, Johannesburg was nothing more than a region of scattered farmlands, but then gold was discovered. It was subsequently found that there was a subterranean, gold-bearing reef that stretched for at least 50 miles, west to east. The city rapidly expanded, and several small towns were established along this strip to service a string of gold mines. Because Johannesburg was a relatively modern city, with the streets laid out in a grid system, there were few old buildings. Just one or two farm or mine houses dating from the 19th century were dotted in and around the neighborhood.

The whole stretch of mining towns is known as the Witwatersrand, which is Afrikaans for "White Water City". The locals sometimes just refer to it as "The Reef". At the time of our arrival there, the population of Johannesburg itself was about three quarters of a million. Later, however, the boundary was expanded to incorporate several African townships, with a combined population of over four million people.

Our exploration plans were somewhat constrained when we discovered that nearly everything closed on a Sunday. Fortunately, this did not include the local zoo, and we managed to navigate our way there using public transport. During its journey, the bus drove down a street lined with Jacaranda trees in full bloom. These are an attractive feature of a number of cities in South Africa, especially Pretoria which, as a consequence, has been nicknamed "The Jacaranda City". In an effort to describe the Jacarandas in a letter to family back in the UK, my wife Susan could only write "They are like bluebells growing in trees."

It was a good choice of venue; the zoo was spacious and with large open areas for many of the animals. After a lengthy walk around the enclosures, we were pleased to find that there was a restaurant, and enjoyed a healthy lunch. Back at our hotel, we reflected on our day and were quite pleased that we had successfully explored some of the city by ourselves, and had used the local buses. There was just one small drawback. We were advised that the Hillbrow area was not a safe place to be walking around at night, and so we spent nearly every evening inside the hotel. Our lodgings had not yet subscribed to the fledgling television service, so we did not even have that to keep us entertained after dark. Still, this was no time for complaining.

Chapter 4

Getting Down to Business

It was Monday morning, and time to start the serious business of making a life for ourselves in this new country. On arrival at the immigration office, it was obvious that there were a dozen or more other immigrants like us there, ready to commence the formalities that bureaucracy demanded. As a group, we were first treated to a welcoming speech by a senior official. He very kindly said how much people like us were needed, and then—somewhat unnecessarily in view of it being free—apologized that the hotel accommodation might not be of the quality we would have liked.

We were each required to apply for an identity document, which would contain all the important detail about the holder. This would include (if applicable) a marriage certificate and South African driving license (issued on proof of a British one), plus confirmation that the individual was classified as a permanent resident. This was popularly referred to as "The Book of Life". Each person would be given an all-important identity number, which would have to be quoted whenever it was requested for official purposes. Once this pep talk was over, we awaited our turns to be interviewed individually.

When the time came to meet my immigration officer, the first thing he said was, "Mister Lowis, what are you doing here in Johannesburg? You should have gone to Durban!" Apparently, each immigrant had been matched with a potential employer, and mine was a large manufacturing conglomerate with a head office in that coastal city. After taking a moment to recover from this opening salvo, my response was that it had been my practice from the start to write to potential employers, to try and secure a job interview. The most promising response had been from a food company based in Johannesburg. He still seemed rather dubious about this, but asked for the name of a person he could telephone. The officer then promptly made the call, whilst I waited, trying not to show any sign of anxiety.

Thankfully, the man on the other end of the line confirmed his interest in seeing me, and an appointment was arranged for a day or two ahead. Now, somewhat pacified, the immigration officer told me to come back and see him again the day after the interview. After covering several other formalities, the meeting came to an end, thankfully without any other surprises.

The visit to the food company's head office was very productive. My meeting was with the managing director of a group of bakeries who, to my delight, immediately offered me a position. The details of the job were not very specific at this time but, in the first instance, I would be seconded to a bread bakery to familiarize myself with the operation there.

At my second meeting with the immigration officer, he seemed to be impressed by the good news, and asked, "What salary will you receive?" On hearing that it would start at 700 South Africa rands a month—which was the equivalent to about 400 hundred British pounds at that time—he jumped up, shook my hand and said, "Many congratulations; this is even more than most artisans receive." Obviously, he was pleased that he would not have to either find me a local job, or insist that my family relocate to Durban. Ah well, if he was happy, then that made two of us. The following Monday, a company driver took me to the bakery located to the east of the city.

The next few weeks were an education for me, not just concerning the company's business, but in the way things were done in South Africa. In order to ensure there was at least one basic foodstuff that was readily available, inexpensive and nutritious, the government had decreed that bakeries must produce what they called a "Standard Loaf". This large, oblong, white bread was made to a prescribed recipe, and it retailed at a controlled price. One popular, novel use for this bread was for "Bunny Chow". This fast food was devised by the Indian community in Durban. Half of a loaf is hollowed out and filled with a curry sauce or whatever takes one's fancy. The crust prevents any leakage of the liquid, and the meal can be scooped out with the fingers and eaten on the move. Many years later, we were amused to see that variations of this were on sale in the UK.

The bakery churned out these loaves day after day. Among the small number of other products made were "Vetkoeks", which is Afrikaans for "Fat Cooks". Like the bread, these were made from flour, salt and yeast. Bun-sized balls of this dough were then deep fried in oil. They could be eaten as they were, or filled with sweet or savory such as jam, meat, or cheese. Like the bread, whilst not providing all the essentials of a healthy diet, for a modest price these products nevertheless filled the bellies of those who were hungry.

The bread was produced using a continuous conveyor-belt system, by a labor force of several dozen African men working in shifts. Many of these were itinerant workers who were housed in small flats within a compound next to the factory. We learned that this was not unusual and, in fact, it was also the way the mines were staffed, as will be discussed in chapter 5. The workers did not have their families with them, but returned home with their accumulated savings at the end of a contract period. In contrast, there were very few senior staff, and these were all white people as might be expected. There was a bakery manager, a production supervisor, an order clerk, an engineer, and two or three office workers. My subsequent experience with other companies confirmed that the labor force in this small factory was a microcosm of the general situation in South African industry, at least during the apartheid years.

Our free immigrant accommodation had come to an end, and we had managed to rent a flat in an attractive, north-western suburb of the city called Florida Hills. We had no sooner moved there when my secondment at the bakery ended. The senior executive who had employed me sent me to a permanent appointment at the town of Springs, 31 miles to the east of Johannesburg. This resulted in a round-trip of about 80 miles each day. As work started at seven-thirty in the morning, which turned out to be the norm in South Africa, this did not allow much time for a morning lie-in! By way of some compensation, at least in the manufacturing industry, it was also a common practice to cease work for the week early on a Friday afternoon. For many in this outdoor country, this was the chance to play golf or enjoy some other sport.

After enduring two or three months of this commuting, we rented a house in a suburb of Springs itself, thereby reducing my commuting time to just a few minutes. Like nearly all dwellings in this part of the world, the house was detached and single-storey, with two bathrooms. Having lived in typical but modest semi-detached houses in the UK, with bedrooms upstairs and just a single bathroom, this was verging on luxury! With plenty of land available in South Africa, gardens were also larger and many had a swimming pool. It would, however, have been too much to expect that our new home would also have this added feature.

The factory was a biscuit bakery employing about 100 people, and was fitted with several long ovens similar to those in my factory back in the UK. These were fitted with conveyor belts, and they baked a wide variety of items. Among these were large army biscuits that serve as iron rations for the armed forces. An inspection of the warehouse revealed that it contained more stocks of these than seemed necessary. Apparently, the factory performance was strongly influenced by how much flour it used—this being purchased from the parent company. Army biscuits used a lot of flour, so logic decreed that many of these were manufactured. The fact that money was tied up with unsold stock did not seem to concern anyone, least of all the head office number crunchers.

The factory had the usual shop-floor African workforce although, unlike the previous bread bakery, this site was located close enough to the township where they lived to eliminate the need for a residential compound. Again, the management and office staff were white men and women. In the country as a whole, however, it was not just a simple case blacks versus whites. In addition to acquainting myself with the job, my learning curve about South African history, customs and culture was also on a steep increase. It became clear that your first language, as well as your racial group, influenced the sector in which you were likely to be employed. For the white population, often also referred to as "Europeans", this would be largely determined by the original country of your ancestors.

In order to better understand some of the less familiar practices we encountered, it may be helpful to sketch in some brief details of how the present day population mix had evolved.

This country was much more of a multi-cultural nation than was first thought. Archaeological finds indicated that prehistoric *Homo sapiens* inhabited the southern part of the African continent. The earliest residents were probably the San people (sometimes referred to by the derogatory term "Bushmen"). These people were hunter-gatherers descended from their Stone Age ancestors, and they date back about 15,000 years. They still exist today in scattered communities, mainly in Namibia. Much later, in approximately 1,000 AD, members of the Karanga tribe drifted down from the northern areas of Africa. Over the next 200 hundred years or so, other groups followed, so that today there are a variety of BaNtu (black) races living in South Africa. It would be erroneous to think of these people as an homogenous population, as they manifest a diverse range of cultures and at least 10 different languages.

So far as is known, the first people of European origin to visit South Africa were Portuguese sailors seeking a trade route to India. Then, in the year 1652, an event of lasting significance for the country took place. It was when Jan van Riebeeck arrived from Holland to establish a command trading outpost at Table Bay. This was regarded as the first permanent colony of white immigrants in South Africa. These settlers were the originators of the present Afrikaners, whose language developed from the Dutch. It is easy to see why, as their ancestors were believed to be the pioneers in bringing European culture and customs to this country, the Afrikaners still felt they had a right to govern it.

The British took possession of the Cape area from 1795 to 1803, and parties of ordinary settlers from that country arrived in the year 1820. It is their descendents, supplemented by more recent immigrants, who today largely make up the English-speaking sector. At the time of our arrival, civil service positions, from Prime Minister to postman and engine driver, were almost exclusively held by Afrikaans speakers. In contrast, most manufacturing, engineering and technical positions, including those at this bakery, were staffed by those whose first language was English.

But the divisions did not end there. For reasons we never quite understood, the greengrocery trade was controlled by people of Portuguese origin, and the corner-shop, convenience stores, by Greeks. Woe betides anybody else who tried to muscle in on these trades! Other immigrants to the country included Indians, who originally came as traders and laborers on the sugar plantations, and settlers from France, Germany, and China. Finally, there were people known as "Colored's", these being of mixed race, who were Afrikaans-speakers. Not only did the black people have their own residential townships, but so did the Indians and Colored's. Thus, the cultural situation was far removed from what outsiders may have regarded as a simple division of blacks and whites.

English and Afrikaans were the two official languages in South Africa, and it might have been expected that the entire population would be bilingual. In order to obtain the school-leaving matriculation certificate, all pupils had to obtain passes in both of these tongues. Although one could only admire those people who were fluent in the two languages, it was often the case that proficiency in their second one was poor. As the Africans were brought up to speak at least one of the many native dialects, they then had the added burden of also having to learn both English and Afrikaans.

Some universities taught exclusively in just one or other of the official languages. The only one that offered parallel tuition was the University of South Africa. In 1877 this was the first institution of higher education in the country to receive a royal charter, which it did from Queen Victoria. In 1946 it became a distance learning university. In due course I was to take full advantage of the opportunity to study at this seat of learning, to help qualify me for a mid-life career change.

We were a little apprehensive: would we be comfortable in this complex "Rainbow Nation", as Nelson Mandela was later to describe it? Would we be accepted, or might even more "pommy immigrants" like us be resented?

There was no reason for us to expect an unconditional welcome from any of the resident population. One derogatory comment that we heard more than once was that you could always tell when a plane full of immigrants had arrived at the airport, because the whining continued after the jet engines had been turned off! Another unflattering term in circulation was "when-we's". This was most often directed at immigrants from what was then Southern Rhodesia, because they were forever saying, "*When we were in Rhodesia, we always did this or that.*" Our little family was determined to avoid pitfalls such as these and, instead, try wholeheartedly to integrate ourselves into the local culture.

We did not systematically set out to learn Afrikaans but, inevitably, came to understand a useful list of words. Partly this was out of necessity. Even though all signs and essential documentation were supposed to be in both official languages, on occasions we would be faced with something only in Afrikaans. For example, it was quite unnerving to be driving along a major road and to be confronted with a sign that stated "Hoe Links". We quickly had to learn that this meant "Keep Left". It was also useful for me to recognize some Afrikaans swear words, partly to be aware of when we were being sworn at (usually good naturedly), but also so that we did not fall into the trap of repeating everything that we heard in polite company.

Despite our initial concerns about whether or not we would be accepted, we did not encounter any animosity. In fact, we were treated very kindly by virtually all with whom we came into contact. This was very gratifying, and touching. We were after all comers-in; our passage and initial accommodation had all been paid for, and we were taking advantage of the work and all that the country had to offer. We were in a more privileged position than the bulk of the population and, as yet, had done nothing to justify anything but perhaps resentment. This was not the case, and we were determined to try and repay this kindness, and put something back into this country for as long as we remained there.

Chapter 5

The Music

HAVE YOU HEARD ANY South African music? The evocative song "Wimoweh" ("The lion sleeps tonight") was written in the Zulu language by Solomon Linda, in 1939, and was featured in Disney's *The Lion King*. Then there was Miriam Makeba who performed many traditional numbers including "The click song". Apart from this being a foot-tapping melody, it was novel for its use of a clicking noise produced at the back of the throat. This sound is a routine part of the language of the Xhosa people, and it is notoriously difficult to reproduce unless one is brought up in this community.

There are also many well-known African jazz musicians, perhaps the most famous being the trumpeter Hugh Masekela. By coincidence, his second wife was Miriam Makeba, but this union was short-lived. One of the other great jazz names was Adolph Johannes "Dollar" Brand, so-called because he used to buy gramophone records from American sailors in Cape Town for a dollar each. Later, he changed his name to Abdulla Ibrahim. He is a pianist, composer and band leader, and his style of music is known as Cape Jazz. In 1959 he formed the "Jazz Epistles", which was the first African jazz band to record a long-playing album. Again by coincidence, one of the original musicians in this group was Hugh Masekela.

It was listening to performers such as these on the radio or in films, along with recordings of gospel choirs, which fuelled my desire to hear indigenous African music in its natural setting. Fossil finds indicate that civilization evolved in Africa and, as music is found in every known culture and historical period, perhaps it also had its origins in this continent. The urge to experience for myself the very roots of music—the language of emotion—was strong.

The first opportunity to hear African choral singing in a naturalistic setting came unexpectedly, during my time at the biscuit factory in Springs. One of the operatives had sadly died, and his colleagues asked if somebody from management would attend the funeral and say a few words about the deceased. None of the other staff members seemed keen on volunteering, but my interest in visiting a township and learning more about local customs encouraged me to offer to attend on their behalf.

The funeral was to be held in Kwa Thema (literally "Thema's place", in the Zulu language) a few miles from the main town. The apartheid government had established townships adjacent to all towns and cities, to ensure the separation of each racial group. It was against the law for white people to enter a township without permission, and to visit one would be a new experience for me. Kwa Thema was established in 1951, and had a population of nearly 100,000, more than half being Zulus.

My guide was a man known to me only as "Longway". His English was good, and he was often the spokesperson for the other workers. On the day of the funeral, and with my portable cassette tape recorder in a carry bag, Longway directed me to the outskirts of Kwa Thema. As was typical of all such townships, a police station was located on the boundary to keep an eye on who was coming and going. Longway said, "Stop here while I go into the station to ask permission for you to enter the township."

Whilst he was gone, doubts crossed my mind—rather belatedly at this late stage. Just what was a naïve, pommy immigrant like me letting himself in for? Here, in a location foreign to me, perhaps the only white person for miles around, it was easy to feel vulnerable to any aggression, robbery, or even a basic resentment for being of the same race as those responsible for enforcing the apartheid regime. Those were the days before the invention of mobile telephones, and probably there would not even be any public phone boxes conveniently dotted around the town. Would this be the time to tell Longway that maybe it was not a good idea after all, and that it would be best to return to familiar territory?

When he returned, commenting, "We can carry on now", my negative thoughts were kept under wraps, at least for the present, and we continued the journey into Kwa Thema.

It was soon apparent that most roads in the township were not surfaced with tarmac or concrete, but were left as compressed dirt or sand. Inevitably, clouds of dust were kicked up by any moving vehicle, and could even be tasted in the air. There was also the constant smell of smoke, as townships were not smokeless zones: coal fires were used for both heating and cooking. After a few minutes, we arrived at the home of the widow. Without anything being said to me, three large ladies squashed themselves into the back seat of my car, and Longway then told me to proceed to the cemetery. Perhaps there was some prestige in the closest family members being chauffeured to the funeral like this and that, unbeknown to me, Longway had organized it. But it would have been nice to have been asked first!

There was a large crowd at the burial site, and it was intriguing to see that the mourners from the biscuit factory all were wearing their work overalls. These were of various colors and had been washed clean. Maybe there was something symbolic in this, such as the workers demonstrating an affiliation with their deceased colleague. The temptation to ask for an explanation at that time was resisted: this was, after all, a funeral, and not lesson in local customs for my benefit.

Nobody else seemed to be speaking English, and Longway's occasional commentaries were my only means of knowing what was going on. He knew of my interest in recording some of the singing, but it was important not to risk offending anyone by appearing disrespectful during this solemn event. The graveside service commenced, and my short eulogy was delivered with Longway translating each sentence into the vernacular. My words seemed inadequate for the occasion, as my knowledge of the deceased was minimal, and about the only suitable thing to say was that he was a respected, hard worker.

The time came when Longway said, "There will be some singing now, and you can record it." A group of the mourners commenced their first of several beautiful but plaintive songs. Nobody seemed to be conducting them, and it was not clear if this was an organized choir or just spontaneous singing. The words were in the local dialect and therefore unintelligible to an outsider like me, but they could have been hymns suitable for a funeral. The melody was unaccompanied, and the usual style was for a single, powerful voice to lead with the first few notes, and then for the rest of the group to join in, singing in a harmony that seemed to come quite naturally. The overall effect was very moving.

When the graveside service was over, Longway guided me out of Kwa Thema and back along the dusty roads, stopping only at the police station to register my departure. This was an opportunity to reflect on my experience over the last hour or two. Contrary to earlier worries, there had been no trouble or threats, although it was difficult to gauge what the locals actually thought of my presence there. Yes, the choral singing, whilst limited in scope, was moving and had not disappointed. In fact, it had wetted my appetite for more.

Sometime later, a group of women at the factory were kind enough to sing a number of songs for me to record. They also explained their meaning. The items all seemed to be rather sad, and the ladies said that most were sung at church. It struck me that the apartheid system, with its many deprivations, had resulted in a preference for singing songs that lamented the situation in which many Africans found themselves. In response to a specific question about whether they were unhappy because of the deprivations they were forced to endure, the ladies said, "Yes, the songs expressed the hope that one day things would be better, and asked for God's help to bring this about."

This made me feel sad too, and confirmed that unequal treatment of human beings for any reason is morally wrong. Music can have a consoling and even a healing function. Singing songs

The Music

that express one's feelings and emotions can bring some degree of comfort, especially when in the company of others who are in the same situation. In due course there would be other opportunities for me to hear more of this type of singing, including during a multi-denominational service in a township church to welcome the new President of the Methodist Conference. Later, whilst being employed by another, larger company, there was even an opportunity for me to organize an inter-departmental choir competition. The judges were two leading members of the Baragwaneth Hospital Choir, in Soweto, famous in South Africa and beyond.

So far, my experience of listening to authentic African music had been largely restricted to the melodic and harmonious components, but there is another very important element: rhythm. This is rooted in nature, and in our biological makeup, for example our breathing and heartbeat. It is also evident in marching, chanting, drumming and other warlike behaviors such as hunting and fighting. Shaka Zulu, who lived from about 1787 to 1828, was largely responsible for developing the Zulu nation into a fighting force to be reckoned with. Rhythmic war dances were a way of both building up courage and aggression in the warriors, and instilling fear and trepidation in the enemy.

The thought entered my mind: can such activities still be seen and heard today? If so, where? It appeared that the places to go were what were known as "Mine Dances". It was mentioned in chapter 3 that there was a string of gold mines along the Witwatersrand. Whilst many of these had long been exhausted, leaving only the characteristic yellow mine dumps of excavated spoil, a few were still active. These were manned by iterant African mine-workers who were hired on fixed-term contracts that embraced most of the calendar year. Like the situation at the bread bakery, during their tenure the men lived in a compound adjacent to the mine. Sometimes on a Sunday, the miners dressed in their traditional costumes and entertained visitors with their singing and dancing. My family was very pleased when a friend at the factory arranged for us to attend one of these shows.

Once again my tape recorder was in action, both to capture some of the sounds and to make comments on what was happening. Listening to it again now does not do justice to the visual spectacle that was a large part of the performance. The miners were dressed in their tribal regalia that included leopard skins, head dresses and various other items including tassels and animal tails. Some performers also carried spears. Their feet were bare, and their legs sometimes had rattles attached below the knees that made a clattering sound when the feet were brought down hard in rhythmic, stamping movements. Commands were occasionally shouted out in "Fanagalo"—a basic language derived from Zulu, English and Afrikaans for use in the mines. It was important that all races and tribes working underground had a lingua franca for safety instructions and essential information.

These dances were accompanied by drum beats, whistles, and shouts of single words or repetitive short phrases. Some items included musical instruments. In one dance, the performers had what resembled small bells attached to a belt strung across their chests. As with the rattles on the legs, the bells jingled with the energetic stamping and jumping. There was also a performance involving a batch of six xylophone-like marimbas that were played with sticks or bones. The musicians appeared to be playing in unison, and their repertoire largely comprised repetitive melodic phrases that suited the instrument. Rather incongruously, however, and perhaps for the benefit of the tourists in the audience, it included versions of the carols "Jingle Bells" and "Silent night". It was not even Christmas time!

Overall, in addition to the rather limited use of music, and apart from drums, the whole performance was very physical, with much leaping and tumbling. It also included a comic item with one man dressed as an elephant pretending to jump into the audience. As it neared the end, the dancing, drumming and shouting became more warlike. This gave those in the audience just a taste of what it must have been like for an opposing army to confront a gathering like this. Not only did the dancing and shouting result in adrenaline-fuelled aggression, but the drawn-out and repetitive

The Music

nature of the dancing and singing might well have had a hypnotic effect on the warriors. In turn, this could result in the banishment of any fear or reluctance to enter into a battle from which they might not emerge alive.

Of course, this mine dance was a performance for an audience, and perhaps also a chance for the dancers to let off some steam and preserve some tribal customs and traditions. The thought crossed my mind: were such war-like activities ever used in anger today? The answer came some years later, when working at a large plastics-molding factory. It was Friday afternoon—payday for the operatives. Unfortunately, a computer in the wages office was giving trouble, and the payroll was not ready in time.

When the workers thought that they would not be paid, they reacted by parading around the factory and offices, singing and stamping in a warlike manner. It was truly spine-tingling to hear this musical chanting gradually growing louder as the "warriors"—for that is what they had now become—approached. Many of the staff locked themselves in their offices, fearing that the situation could turn physically aggressive. There was some sort of compromise that partly defused the situation, the details of which are now forgotten, but it was an experience that one would not wish to be repeated in a hurry.

South African music was not restricted to the traditional "black" genre, but it also included some distinctive "white" and "fusion" varieties. Eve Boswell, whilst being of Hungarian descent, spent much of her life in South Africa and was also a popular performer in England. Her hit songs included "Sugar Bush", sung partly in Afrikaans, and "Pickin' a chicken". These had a novel rhythm that at least partly reflected a style developed by the European settlers, and especially the Afrikaners, known as "Boeremusiek". This folk music was played by small groups with a distinctive concertina lead, along with guitars, a banjo and a bass. It comes across as light and cheerful dance music, with an infectious rhythm that encourages everyone to join in.

The urban African population developed "Township jazz" that combined Traditional beats with more westernized melodies.

It was usually performed with a saxophone lead, accompanied by rhythm instruments. Several varieties were recognized, one being "Kwela" that uses penny whistles playing repetitive melody lines. The catchy tune "Tom Hark" is a Kwela number that became a hit in many countries.

The repressive apartheid policy made it difficult, indeed dangerous, for musicians of different races to play together. Nevertheless, as with the pioneers in the USA that defied the segregationalist policy, so did some courageous people in South Africa. In 1969 guitarist Johnny Clegg teamed up with a number of black musicians to form a multi-ethnic band called "Juluka", but they were forced to keep a low profile. Clegg was arrested and beaten up by police on a number of occasions in the early days. The authorities eventually had to be more tolerant, and must have been influenced by the commercial success of the musical "Ipi Tombi" (a corruption of the Zulu for "where is the girl?") in the mid-1970s. Ironically, although this was performed by black artists, it was written by Bertha Egnos and her daughter Gail Lakier—both white! During the interval, Johnny Clegg performed with his band.

It was both inevitable and desirable that a style of music would develop that combined the African and European formats. One of the most successful contemporary, or "Afropop", outfits was an 11-piece, non-racial group called "Mango Groove". They formed in 1984, had many hits in South Africa, and made several overseas tours. Their repertoire includes some Kwela, some haunting ballads, and many upbeat foot-tappers including "Special Star". This dynamic number starts with a solo penny whistle, builds to a rhythmic crescendo, and concludes with a reprise that brings an exciting close to many of their live concerts.

Indeed, South African music in all its forms has a lot to offer, and deserves more recognition than it has had. When we emigrated, my eager anticipation of hearing some good indigenous music was rewarded many times over by the quality and variety that we experienced in those 20 years—and it continues to give pleasure through my own tapes and commercial recordings.

Chapter 6

Rhodesia and Lesotho

AFRICA IS, OF COURSE, not just one country but a whole continent that contains at least 54 sovereign nations. What is generally referred to as Southern Africa comprises 15 countries, and South Africa borders on six of them. To the north is Botswana and Rhodesia (as it was known then), to the east is Mozambique, and to the west is South West Africa (now called Namibia). The Kingdom of Lesotho is entirely within South Africa, and Swaziland partly shares its boundaries with Mozambique.

In addition to these sovereign states, during the apartheid era the government created "Homelands", with limited self-rule for various black tribal groups, probably to justify the continued white domination of the rest of the country. These included Transkei, Ciskei, Venda, and Bophuthatswana. In reality, this policy was not as magnanimous as it may seem. The land quality and resources of these regions were generally poor, and there was little or no established industry. The local populations were probably no better off there than in the rest of the country.

An exception was Bophuthatswana, where entrepreneur Sol Kerzner had built the casino and entertainment centre he called Sun City. Situated only about two hours drive from Johannesburg, people visited in large numbers to gamble, which was illegal in South Africa, and to see artists who would not perform to segregated audiences. The Homelands were abolished in 1994, when the new democratic constitution became operative.

Forever the proverbial tourists, we were determined to experience as much of this part of the world as we could, during what we thought would be the two or three years of our residence there. Would life be much the same in these neighboring states as it was in South Africa? This chapter describes our visits to two of these countries, and chapter 8 will chronicle the experiences we had in another three of them.

The political situation in Rhodesia was potentially unstable at that time, so we decided to visit Victoria Falls at the first opportunity, whilst it was still considered safe to do so. After Northern Rhodesia gained independence in 1964 and was renamed Zambia, the southern nation that remained as a British colony became simply "Rhodesia". Negotiations with the UK government the following year, to give power to the majority black population there, broke down. In defiance, Prime Minister Ian Smith announced a Unilateral Declaration of Independence (UDI). Economic sanctions of varying intensity were imposed on the country in 1965, and these lasted until 1979; they were therefore still in place when we planned our visit.

In April 1976, just six months after our arrival, we boarded an Air Rhodesia aircraft for the 100-minute flight to this famous natural wonder. We thought that it would be exciting to see the falls from the air. Fortunately, the flight-path to the landing strip just allowed us just a quick glimpse of the billowing spray beneath us, and the chance for a "point and press" photograph through the airplane window. Once landed, it was just a few minutes shuttle-bus ride to the Victoria Falls Hotel, and a short walk from there to the falls themselves.

Eager to waste no time, and armed with camera and cassette recorder, we made our way along the path to the banks of the Zambezi River, and then followed it down past various parts of the waterfall. The terrain changed into a rain forest, formed due to the constant falling of spray that was being driven 350 feet into the air by the immense amount of water cascading down the falls. We were soaked to the skin!

Rhodesia and Lesotho

Looking back, we could see the famous Victoria Falls Bridge that linked Rhodesia with Zambia. It was in a train on this bridge, just eight months previously, that talks had taken place between Prime Minister Ian Smith and various Rhodesian nationalist delegates, along with the Zambian and South African presidents acting as mediators, to try and find a path toward democratic rule. These talks failed, just like those with the British government had done several years previously.

This would be a good time to start the cassette recorder and ask the boys what they thought of the falls. With the roar of the waterfall almost drowning out his voice, David said, "Look! There is a rainbow caused by the spray."

Peter then added, "We have just walked past the 'Devil's Cataract', the 'Rainbow Falls', and then the 'Horseshoe Falls'. You can get very close to them." When asked what the local people had called the waterfalls from the earliest of times, Peter remembered that it was: "The smoke that thunders."

The boys were clearly excited by the spectacle, and it had lived up to its expectations. Whilst the Victoria Falls is not the highest, or widest, waterfall in the world, when both height and width are taken jointly taken into consideration, it is the largest falls in existence. When we had had our fill of gazing at this spectacle from various vantage points, it just remained for us to trudge back to the hotel to change out of our sopping clothes.

The next day we hired a car and went on the local game drive. Unfortunately, the best trail would have been along the banks of the Zambezi River, but this was closed for security reasons. Nevertheless, the 15-mile trail we followed through the African bush was enjoyable, although somewhat sparse on game. When we could go no further and took a short break before turning back, it was an opportunity to ask the boys what they thought of this. Peter said, "We could see two zebra, some hyenas, and also some wild boar." However, on the return drive, he recorded a rather scary incident. We had stopped for a moment, having sighted a large animal in the distance. "An elephant seemed to be coming for us," Peter said excitedly. "It was lucky that we could drive on and leave it behind us."

On the third day we paid a visit to a craft village, no doubt established so that tourists could witness some "authentic" African culture. The local guide was very informative, and we learned that the dominant tribal group there was the Matabele, formed when a group broke away from Shaka Zulu and travelled northwards. He explained that their traditional weapon was the assegai, a short thrusting spear with a blade as long as the warrior's chest is wide.

Outside one of the shops, there was a group of musicians playing marimbas of varying sizes. This evocative music, which we had first heard at a mine dance, sounded just right in these authentic surroundings. Of course we could not resist buying some souvenirs, including a drum and two small African pianos that are held in the hand and played with the thumbs. We later used these in an attempt to record our own version of a traditional song, complete with warlike whoops and shrieks. It was just as well the locals could not hear us!

Before we departed for our return flight, we shared our thoughts on this brief experience of life in Rhodesia. We agreed that the white population, which comprised only about five percent of the total, seemed to be blindly hanging on to the old colonial attitudes and way of life. Despite the economic sanctions and world-wide condemnation, they appeared to be oblivious of the change that had to come sooner or later. For the present, superficial peace was only preserved due to the conscription of white males into the armed forces. This situation was brought home to me some three years later, when my business travels took me to Bulawayo—Rhodesia's second-largest city.

In 1979, during the first of these visits, an attempt had been made to demonstrate some progress toward political change. Bishop Abel Muzorewa had been appointed as Prime Minister of an interim government, and the country had been renamed Zimbabwe-Rhodesia. There was, however, considerable opposition to this from within the country. In less than a year there would be full democratic elections; Canaan Banana would be President, Robert Mugabe Prime Minister, and the "Rhodesia" half of the country's name would disappear.

In talking to people during my visits to audit the Bulawayo subsidiary of the pharmaceuticals company I then worked for, it was apparent that the white population seemed to be resigned to eventual majority rule, but had concerns—real or imagined—that the Africans would not be able to cope with the technology associated with our business. A typical comment made at a blood transfusion centre was, "The blacks won't be able to do this when they take over." It did not seem to strike the speaker that a bit of training now to help them to cope, would be useful.

On one visit to the Bulawayo plant, accompanied by a colleague from our office in South Africa, we were invited to dinner at the home of the factory manager. When we were all seated around the dining table, the lady of the house rang a small hand bell. A black servant in a white uniform came in with the first course. When this was over, she rang the bell again and the servant returned to clear the dishes and bring in the second course. Although my colleague was a South African, we both inwardly squirmed at being waited on in such a feudal manner. This was something you saw in films, not in real life.

Continuing with our desire to see as many southern African countries as possible—even before exploring all the major cities in South Africa itself—we decided to spend Christmas 1976 in the Kingdom of Lesotho. Sometimes known as the "Mountain Kingdom", this is home to about two million Southern Sotho people, and is completely encircled by South Africa. It was the British protectorate of Basutoland until 1966, when it gained independence and adopted its current name.

The main hotel in the country was a Holiday Inn in the capital, Maseru. This was a popular venue for South Africans, who were no doubt enticed by the legalized gambling, along with the relaxed attitude to mild pornography and Sunday trading that was permitted in that country. Such indulgences were strictly banned in puritanical South Africa, as was any form of entertainment, which included the showing of films on the religious day of rest. On Christmas Day we were entertained by about 20 children, who performed traditional singing and dancing, helped by adults playing drums. Listening to the recordings again now, the music and rhythm, whilst spirited, does seem very repetitive to a European ear.

We saw little sign of development or prosperity during our drive through the countryside to view some ancient rock paintings. All but the main roads in the capital were gravel surfaced, and there appeared to be little industry except for traditional crafts. We drove past small farms with just a few animals, and photographed a farmer tilling the land using a simple wooden plough pulled by two oxen. At another point, we were treated to the novel spectacle of women washing their clothes in a river. There was a worrying moment when it seemed like a local car driver was trying to force us off the dirt road and down a slope. Perhaps there was some animosity here toward "privileged" white people for what was happening in South Africa. Although most residents were friendly and polite, we did also see an occasional sign of this resentment in the hotel.

It was just a short walk from where we parked the car to the rock shelter at Ha Baroana that contained the paintings. The attendant on duty sprayed water on the rock surface to help sharpen up the images. What we saw appeared to be a hunting scene that included large, buffalo-like animals painted in dark red, ochre and white, and spindly images of people. It is always difficult to determine the age of rock art, but these could have been created hundreds or even thousands of years ago by San ("Bushmen") artists. Having previously only seen examples of cave art in books, to view them now "in the flesh" produced a tingle of excitement. What would life have been like for the artists? Why did they wish to create such images? Was there perhaps some religious significance in the paintings?

As we drove back to our hotel, we agreed that seeing these historic images had made a fitting climax to our visit to this kingdom. We would shortly be returning back to our home in South Africa, but we were becoming addicted to exploring new places and seeing things far removed from what we had been used to in England. We now had to return to work, earn some money, and await the next holiday break. Nevertheless, during homeward drive, we were already thinking about what would be our next trip.

Chapter 7

Taking Stock

It was now May, 1976, and we had been in the country for seven months. Whilst we were still very much newcomers, this was a long enough time to have accumulated some knowledge and experience of our adopted country. It was appropriate to take stock of our situation and reflect on our feelings whilst these were still fresh, and before we became so acclimatized that novelty became too commonplace to notice.

After living for three months in the rented house in Springs, in April 1976 we bought our own property in the town of Benoni, which was about half way between Springs and Johannesburg. The name "Benoni" is taken from Genesis, 35:2, and was given to Rachel's newborn son just before she died. It means "son of my sorrow". Whilst one can understand why this might have been meaningful for Rachel's family, we never found out why our town should have been given this name.

The boys had not been happy with the school they attended in Springs. It resulted in a profound cultural shock when compared with their school in England. The teaching system there was very formal, mostly using a "talk and chalk" format, rather than the more creative and explorative system they were used to back in the UK. Although this was a bilingual country, each town appeared to be predominantly either English or Afrikaans, not only in preferred language but also in culture. Springs was clearly in the latter camp, which only added to the officious nature of the school there. When we were able to transfer the boys to a school in Benoni—a town, and school, with a more English lifestyle—they were very relieved.

It might appear ungracious to criticize my employers. The job had provided opportunities to visit their depots in other towns, which enabled me to see more of the country at their expense. It had, however, quickly become clear that the management and organization at the biscuit factory was a rather haphazard affair. There was little systematic planning of what to make, and the decision was usually left to the factory manager who, by coincidence, was also a British immigrant. Written procedures for manufacturing the different products, and the quality specifications, seemed minimal at best. Thus, worried about the ability to justify my salary, here was an opportunity to start compiling a manual that would contain all the essential criteria for the complete product range. This did at least give me the feeling of doing something useful, but it is doubtful that my efforts were taken seriously by anyone else, especially after I had left the company.

The personnel structure at this factory was the same as seen previously, with all senior and administrative staff being white, and the laboring and semi-skilled workers black. Apart from this obvious division, little sign of apartheid in action was evident on the shop floor. The men and women generally went about their tasks cheerfully, and perhaps they were just happy to have a regular job. The wages of the senior blacks were already similar to those of the more junior whites and, to try and close the gap still further, their percentage annual increases were double that of the management and office staff. Unemployment among the Africans was relatively high, and each day there were about a dozen men waiting at the gate in the hope of obtaining some casual work. They were called in if, for example, there was a truck to unload, and were paid an hourly rate for this.

Outside of the factory environment, the apartheid system was all too obvious. As was mentioned in chapter 5, the townships were segregated, but so also were the buses, trains, taxis and public toilets. Cinemas and theatres were for whites only, except for the rare occasion when a show was performed just for a black audience. Many official buildings had separate entrances for the two races, and post offices usually had segregated counters.

Although there were shops in the main towns that catered specifically for traditional African food and clothing, no enforced segregation occurred in the retail centers. Black people could visit the white housing areas to work, as gardeners or domestic servants, but they could only live there if the house had purpose-built servant's quarters. This typically had a single, small room, and a separate toilet, with a cold tap outside. Only a few had electricity. When we bought our own house in Benoni, we had to sign an affidavit in front of a solicitor to confirm that we were white.

So far as we were aware, all houses in black townships were rented from the local municipality. A law that, to us, seemed to be particularly punitive was the "Immorality Act". It was in force to prevent any chance of intimate activity between the races that could ultimately result in mixed-race children. The prohibitions were taken to a ridiculous extreme, such as prohibiting a black woman from sitting next to a white man driving a car—she had to be in the back seat on her own. This vindictive measure reared its head when we went to the multi-denominational church service in the black township, mentioned in chapter 5. Although permission had been given for members of white churches to attend, our group found itself sitting together in the best seats. When we asked why we could not all sit together, we were told that the law prohibited it. This was very sad; we were the outsiders, but it was the locals who had to literally take the back seat.

A question that kept recurring to us concerned the extent to which the resident African population accepted the apartheid situation. How did they really feel about it, deep down in their hearts and minds? There was, understandably, some reluctance to talk about this, which could have been due to a fear of being reported to the authorities for expressing rebellious views. When the ladies at the factory sang their religious songs for me, and were then asked if the rather melancholy emotion these expressed was a reflection of how they felt about life, they answered in the affirmative (see chapter 5). Despite what their innermost feelings might have been, however, the outward appearance and behavior of most black people was invariably cheerful. Was this just a front they put on, to keep out of trouble?

During our brief visit to Victoria Falls (chapter 6), we had detected a different attitude among the local population. Most of the blacks we met there, apart from the guide at the craft village, who was obviously on his best behavior, had a "mean and hungry" look about them. They appeared to be more agitated and impatient for change, as if they wanted to tell the world: "You just wait until we are in power." Minority rule in Rhodesia was maintained by a white population comprising less than five percent of the total, compared with nearly 20 percent at that time in South Africa.

We started to wonder if a democratic style of leadership did not come easily to Africans. The tribes that had been the most successful, for example the Zulus, had achieved this through having a strong, autocratic chief—in this case, Shaka. Whilst he had increased the power of the tribe, and its ability to defeat invading forces, he had done little to generate social advancement for the majority. Any opposition to the chief from within the tribe was dealt with as ruthlessly as were the enemies from outside. In the present day, perhaps those who had a regular job, a home and family, and could live in peace even as second-class citizens, were content to accept the disadvantages along with the benefits. Alternatively, maybe they were just waiting patiently, knowing that change would have to come one day.

In 1976, a black colleague confided in me that he predicted there would be a revolt within five years, if no progress had been made toward majority rule. If and when this time came, however, would there be democracy, or a return to a tribal autocracy system? As will be discussed in later chapters, serious riots occurred in that very year, although it took much longer for democracy to be achieved.

What was puzzling was the reluctance of the black people to accept more responsibility, use initiative, and make efforts to attain more senior positions. Those who already had some authority were hesitant to use it with conviction. My two attempts to give bright workers from the shop floor some additional training, and place them in more advanced jobs, had failed. There was initial enthusiasm and effort, but it is likely that peer pressure then forced the individuals to pull out of the arrangement. It seemed very important to the black workers that they were all on an equal footing, and could not be divided, or seen to be cooperating with the white oppressors. Being equal and united was presumably a nationally agreed strategy, and such solidarity was one of the few defenses against the extremes of the apartheid system.

Security in the country was maintained partly by the visible presence of an armed police force, and partly by plain-clothed special constables and Secret Service personnel. If the situation demanded it, strategically placed army stations could quickly supply additional resources. There was also a separate force of traffic police, whose officers were armed and obviously trained to intervene where necessary. We strongly suspected that there were many pairs of eyes looking for any sign of political agitation, and that any perpetrators would be dealt with swiftly and efficiently.

What could have become something of a joke, had it not been so serious, was the increasing number of banning orders. During the darkest times, hardly a day seemed to pass without us hearing on the radio that a particular organization, gathering, practice or behavior was immediately banned, and: "Would not be tolerated." This phrase has lived with our family ever since and, if there is something we do not like, we try to adopt an Afrikaans accent and say: "It will not be tolerated!" This invariably results in gales of spontaneous laughter.

Having just recently bought our first house, we had to get used to some living conditions that were new to us. In particular, there was the need to have burglar bars fitted to all opening windows in the home, and security gates to every outside door. Without these, the insurance companies would not insure the house. Because these embellishments were the norm, we eventually ceased to be aware of them. During the occasions when we came back to the UK for visits, the fact that suburban homes did not look like miniature prisons was strikingly obvious. It was necessary to be constantly aware of potential robberies, thefts and car high-jackings, and to take all necessary precautions. For many, this included owning and carrying a firearm, and more will be said about this in a later chapter.

Like many typical Brits, in our letters to friends and relatives in the UK we just had to discuss the weather. This part of the country had a very characteristic climate. The winter spans the months of June to August, and these are completely dry and cloudless, with a constant blue sky. The gardens turn brown, and everything looks dead. However, the plant varieties are bred for their ability to withstand this drought, and the lawns are grown from a tough type of grass that has to be planted in tufts by hand. The dry period can extend until November, when it is broken by very violent thunderstorms late in the afternoon, after which it usually remains dry until the same thing occurs again the following day. It was a very rare event when, just once during our time there, it snowed, but this was gone by the next morning.

Something of which we only became aware during our first winter was that the houses did not have central heating, and nor were they well insulated against the cold. At a height of 6,000, the air in the Highveld is thinner than at sea level. Not only did new residents have to acclimatize to the reduced oxygen level but, during the winter, the temperature fluctuates wildly. For an hour or so around mid-day it would be warm but, just a few hours later, the thermometer would indicate that it was below freezing. For many, the only way to keep warm was to go to bed early, and have an electric blanket that was designed to be left on through the night. There was no piped gas supply, at least not in the suburbs. Most heating was by electricity, although oil, bottled gas, or smokeless coal appliances could also be bought.

At a latitude of about 26 degrees south, our location was half the distance to the equator than is, for example, London. Consequently, the sun set early in the evening even in summer. For a country that valued its outdoor activities, this was a restriction, and we wondered why the clocks were not put forward in springtime, as they are in the UK and other countries. Many houses had outdoor swimming pools and, in the warmer months, it was common to have friends round for a swim and barbeque under floodlights, when it was dark.

Our family then discussed what were the worst and the best things we had experienced in this short time. Worst of all was the Afrikaner bureaucracy. Dealing with any official, or professional person such as a solicitor, was slow, inefficient and often unpleasant. We were warned to allow plenty of additional time for completing essential tasks, such as paying vehicle road tax or buying a television license. It took a whole year for our application for a telephone to be processed. Being forewarned is, of course, being forearmed. There was no other option than to take a deep breath and be resigned to the fact that hours would go by when dealing with officialdom, and that the mission may not even be accomplished.

In the UK and other developed countries, during the long dark evenings a person could remain snug indoors and relax in front of the television set. When we arrived in South Africa, the fledging television service only broadcast four hours a night, with the language evenly split between English and Afrikaans. Because of international sanctions, many countries would not sell programs to South Africa, and some of those that were available were dubbed into Afrikaans. Drive-in cinemas were popular, and they at least partly filled the evening entertainment gap. Added to this, our large local church showed films on a regular basis for a modest fee, which included refreshments.

We were, of course, very uncomfortable with the apartheid situation. Change had to come one day and, hopefully, this would not be too far in the future. Whilst it was difficult for us to influence government policy—we did not even have the right to vote—we could be as kind, considerate and helpful as possible toward those unfortunate victims of this inhumane practice.

Concluding now to the best things we had experienced so far, the obvious attractions had been visiting new places, experiencing a different culture, exploring the African flora and fauna, and hearing traditional music. South Africans were very outdoor oriented, enjoying sports, swimming, and barbeques. The comments made on our boat journey that the three most important things in this country were: "Sunny skies, braaivleis and rugby" was proving correct. A different sort of event that clearly stood out as a highlight for me was attending the very moving church service in the local township of Kwa Thema.

Despite the problems we had encountered, we had no regrets about our decision to emigrate. We wondered if this initial euphoria of being tourists and experiencing so many new things would eventually wear off, and that life would become dull and mundane. Only time would tell.

Chapter 8

Swaziland, SWA, and Botswana

WERE ALL THE COUNTRIES in Southern Africa much the same, or would there be significant differences? Certainly one could expect that the climate at these latitudes would not be influenced by mere geographical boundaries, and neither would the flora and fauna if left to its own devices. What could be different was the socio-political situation, based on whether or not the country had achieved independence. We had already experienced signs of increasing tension in Rhodesia under extreme minority rule, but then some animosity toward Europeans still existed in independent Lesotho.

Of the remaining countries bordering on South Africa, there were concerns about the security situation in Mozambique that discouraged us from visiting it. After many years of conflict, independence from Portugal had been achieved in June 1975. All the remaining Portuguese settlers had been expelled. The land that once used to be a favored holiday haunt, especially for people in the Transvaal, for whom it was the shortest drive to the sea, became an unwelcome place to be. With Mozambique off the list, this left Swaziland, Botswana and what was then called South West Africa—now Namibia—for us to explore.

Swaziland was a British protectorate until it achieved full independence in the year 1968. In contrast to Lesotho, which is completely encircled by South Africa, part of Swaziland shares borders with Mozambique. This is politically advantageous to the small kingdom, as it does not have to rely exclusively on the goodwill of South Africa for an overland route to the sea.

We visited the kingdom of Swaziland in February, 1977, when Susan's parents were spending a holiday with us. The million or so population there is made up of several tribal groups. After driving past some road-side stalls selling traditional crafts and souvenirs, we made our way to the small town of Mbabane, the country's capital. Compared with Maseru, this had some modern buildings, as well as indoor and outdoor markets. What immediately struck us was that, in contrast to Lesotho, where most journeys were upwards into the hills, here we were heading downwards toward the heart of the country. This low-lying terrain seemed to trap the heat, and it was uncomfortably hot.

We again stayed at a Holiday Inn, which was located just outside of the town, and visited the outdoor swimming pool as often as we could to try and cool off. When we later recorded our impressions, Susan remarked, "It was a lovely setting, with mountains all around us. There were not many people in traditional dress, and the service in the hotel was rather lethargic—it needed a bit more supervision." As was the case in Lesotho, there was a hint of some resentment toward white visitors like us. My attempt to photograph a scene in the open market, that included craftsman working with metal, resulted in stones being thrown in my direction.

The Milwani game reserve was just a short drive away from where we were staying. Although though not large, this was a very attractive location, and the park was well stocked with animals. We looked down on a lake shimmering with the reflection of the blue sky and fluffy white clouds above. It was surrounded by African grassland, and scattered trees with their branches of green leaves swaying gently in the breeze. This, set against a mountain backdrop, brought out the artist in me and made me wish for the skill to record this scene on canvass. With the absence of both the equipment and ability, however, a memorable photograph had to suffice.

We rested in a viewing hide, and were treated to the sight of a hippopotamus leisurely swimming in a pool very close to us. A short time later, three graceful giraffe came near to the hide and paid their respects to us. These views of natural African scenery and wildlife provided photographs and memories for Susan's parents to take back home with them. Our own recollections are still triggered by a large mohair wall-hanging that we bought just before we left Swaziland. It depicts images of people and animals similar to what we saw in the Lesotho rock paintings, and we were introduced to a girl called Elizabeth, who had woven it. Yes, Swaziland was a nice place to visit.

The large geographical area of what was then called South West Africa is sparsely populated, with only about a million people living there during our time in the region. These comprise various ethnic groups, between them speaking 12 languages including English, Afrikaans and German. Its political history is complex. The country became a German protectorate in 1884 but, during the First World War, South Africa took over its occupation. A formal mandate to administer this territory was granted to them by the League of Nations in 1920. Despite subsequent internal pressure to relinquish control, South Africa resisted until full independence was achieved in the year 1990. At this time, the country was renamed "Namibia". Interestingly, the coastal enclave of Walvis Bay was excluded from this for a further four years, and it remained under South African control.

When Susan took our two youngest children (we now had an addition to the family, see chapter 13) back to the UK for a short holiday in April, 1979, it afforded an ideal opportunity for me to take my eldest son, Peter, on a trip to South West Africa. The trip would involve long hours of driving, and some accommodation that might not have been very suitable for our latest family addition, then aged just 21 months, and David who was 10 years old.

Travelling by car due west was not practical for an ordinary family car, due to the absence of suitable roads. Our route therefore took us firstly on the long road south to Upington on the Orange River, a distance of approximately 445 miles. After an overnight stay and an early start the next day, we then headed west before turning northwards to enter South West Africa through its southern boundary.

Before reaching the camp that would be our destination for the next few nights, we left the main road and joined a dirt track to visit the "Roaring Dune". This was a massive sand dune that apparently made this roaring noise when a strong wind blew across its top. Because of this, it was also continually changing its shape and position. What was interesting was that the dune was made up of sands of different colors but, no matter how much these moved around due to the action of the wind, the grains remained separated. No doubt the experts would be able to give an explanation for this remarkable phenomenon.

Later in the day we arrived at the resort of Ai-Ais, which means "burning water" in the local language. This was a region of extinct volcanoes, and the existence of hot, sulphurous springs in the area was no doubt responsible for its local name. The camp was situated in a valley surrounded by black, rather bleak-looking, volcanic rocks. At the time of our visit, the accommodation included fixed, army-style tents for those like us on a limited budget, with an ablution block close by. Although we cooked most of our meals on our own camping stove, an on-site restaurant provided a welcome change. Thankfully, there was also a large swimming pool to help us cool down in the oppressive heat. Recently, when chatting to Peter about this trip, he said he remembered me forgetting to pack my aftershave lotion, and having to use whisky instead. His memory is better then mine, but such hardships were the stuff of rugged explorers like us, and we bore them bravely.

The scenery in this part of the country can best be described as stark and rugged, rather than lush and pastoral, and this is what attracted a steady stream of visitors. A major geographical attraction was the Fish River Canyon. This large natural feature is among the world's most spectacular examples of its kind, and is the largest in Africa. In order to obtain the best view, we drove up to high ground so that we could look down on a double bend of this deep valley. Like a tiny sliver of silver at the bottom ran the narrow river that, eons ago, must have been a mighty torrent in order to carve out this massive cleft. For athletic types who were fit enough, and had a medical certificate to prove it, it was a challenge to spend several days walking the length of the canyon.

A few days later, we set off northwards to our final destination, Hardap Dam. Essential diversions along the way for the eager explorer were, firstly, the Kokerboom Forest and, secondly, the "Finger of God". The former could easily have been something one might imagine originated from an alien planet, comprising as it did, clusters of strange-looking kokerboom trees. Their branches all pointed to the heavens like the fingers of an upturned hand, with some leathery-looking leaves only on the tips. The name translates as "quiver tree", but it is actually a species of aloe: *Aloe dichotoma*. Legend has it that the local San people used the hollowed-out branches to make quivers for their arrows.

The "Finger of God" is a slim column of sandy rock on a very narrow base, standing on a small hill. It was aptly named because it did look like a massive raised finger, and the fact that it was still standing seemed to defy gravity. Apparently the shape is due to erosion over millennia, and the very bottom of the column has eroded more quickly. It is inevitable that the base will eventually become so thin that the massive finger will topple.

At Hardap Dam we had indoor accommodation, and were able to relax next to this large expanse of water for a couple of days, where Peter tried his hand at fishing. A lovely photograph of the sun setting over the lake, with one or two unusual trees in the foreground, brings back memories of this part of our holiday. It was then another very early start for our journey back home, so early that we had to wait for a petrol station to open, in order to fill up. The drive back, with one overnight break, was about 900miles, which emphasized to us just how big the country is, compared with the UK. As one colleague put it, "It's a large chunk of real estate!"

This was not my only visit to South West Africa, as an opportunity arose for a business trip some five years later. The flight took me to the town of Windhoek (Afrikaans for "Windy Corner"), the capital of the country. After completing my audit of the warehouse there, the manager said that he was going to drive to Walvis Bay to visit a client. As there was not very much to see in Windhoek, this was a great opportunity to join him on his trip. Because of mountains in the way, the road journey of nearly 250 miles requires a detour to the north. On the final stretch we entered the ancient Namib Desert, stopping briefly to photograph a traction engine called "Old Luther", abandoned long ago by the side of the road. When we reached the Skeleton Coast, so-called because of the number of shipwrecks that had occurred there, we turned south at the holiday resort of Swakopmund and headed for Walvis Bay.

The desert stretches right to the sea, and the high sand dunes lined the side of the road for most of this part of the journey. This was my first experience of a genuine, completely barren desert, and a sudden urge developed. The temptation to ask my colleague to stop for a few minutes, to allow me the opportunity to run up the dunes like an excited child, was too strong to resist. At the top, the view across endless miles of golden, rolling dunes was dramatic, generating a feeling that it had been the same since the dawn of time. Whilst this had generated a tingling feeling for me, a pelican that had settled close by for a rest seemed relatively underwhelmed by the magnificent desolation.

The German influence in the architecture was there to see, for example the Altes Amtsgericht building in Swakopmund, which was built in 1906. This large, gable-ended building was painted in a mustard-yellow color, attractively edged in white at the corners and around windows and doors. It had started off as a school, but then became a magistrate's court—from which the present German name derives, and later it was taken over as municipal offices. Walvis Bay itself is a fishing port, and several large boats were anchored in the harbor. When we stopped for a refreshment break on the drive back to Windhoek, there was an opportunity to photograph two Herero women in their traditional long dresses, which are made up of many layers of material. Although the Herero people played an important role in the early history of South West Africa, they currently numbered only about seven percent of the population.

Two years later, in April 1981, the whole family embarked on a short holiday to the last of the neighboring countries. This

Swaziland, SWA, and Botswana

time it was Botswana, which was called Bechuanaland before it achieved independence from Britain in 1966. Unfortunately, we did not have the opportunity to see any of the famous game reserves, such as the Chobe National Park, or the Okavango Delta. Instead, our brief trip was confined to a narrow eastern strip just over the border from South Africa, which included the capital Gaborone. Compared with our other trips, there is less of note to report about this one.

Yes, we had a nice hotel, saw the African bush, dirt roads, traditional huts, and road-side stalls selling food and crafts. One evening the hotel put on a memorable outdoor barbeque under the stars. This al fresco dining experience in the warm air and with the stars twinkling above, was quite magical. Unfortunately, however, my lasting memory is of catching tick bite fever when we went to see some more rock paintings. It was only explained later that walking through long grass whilst wearing shorts was not a good idea, as ticks lurk in the undergrowth. Luckily, the symptoms did not develop until after we had returned home, and were then only recognized when a work colleague correctly identified the cause of large red blotches on my left leg. Fortunately, the disease responds well to treatment with modern antibiotics.

Apart from the simple pleasure of sightseeing, our desire to visit other southern African countries had been prompted by an interest in exploring any socio-cultural differences. We had encountered some signs of animosity in Rhodesia, Lesotho and Swaziland, even though such behavior may not have been commonplace. We had not noticed this in Botswana, and we had had little interaction with the sparse local population in South West Africa to form an opinion. Each of the countries we visited had potential as tourist destinations, and in some cases this was already being developed. Generating more income from tourism would help to counter the poverty saw all too often.

With all this interest in visiting our neighbors, however, it was time to make amends and further explore our home country of South Africa itself.

Chapter 9

The Animals

No doubt what brings most tourists to South Africa is the chance to see wild animals in their natural habitat. It certainly is a great country for this, and we took full advantage of the opportunities to see all the game parks and the nature reserves that we could during our stay. Holidays to these locations from England, and probably most other countries outside Africa, are expensive and now rather commercialized. For residents like us at that time, they afforded the chance to take a holiday break without spending much money.

For a day out, or even just an afternoon, there were also interesting places to visit nearer home. Not all wild animals are big, fierce man-eaters, so it may be appropriate to start this account of South African fauna at the lowest end of the danger scale, and then work upwards. Just around the corner from where we lived, was Rynfield Bunny Park. This was an area where rabbits scampered freely, along with some sheep and geese. If they could be caught, the animals usually let children pet and cuddle them. Whilst the bunnies did not quite make it into the list of top five game animals, for which Africa is famous, the park was a delightful place, especially for youngsters. It is also held a personal memory for us, as it was where, in August, 1978, our youngest son, Charles, took his first unaided steps, aged 14 months.

The Animals

The next attraction, situated between Johannesburg and Pretoria at a location appropriately called "Halfway House", was a place where cuddling the animals was not recommended. This was the Snake Park, which housed examples of all the slithery reptiles that were native to the country. It included snake-handling and "milking" demonstrations by rangers far braver then we were! There was a more serious aspect to this, however, as the venom extracted from the poisonous species was used to produce the all-important antidotes to otherwise potentially fatal bites.

Moving further up the scale of animal size, there was Johannesburg Lion Park. This was in a very naturalistic setting, and very spacious. Whilst obviously not the same as a natural game reserve, especially as cars had to drive through a double security gate to see the big cats, it nevertheless made for a pleasant day out. There were also native huts to visit, a miniature train ride to enjoy, plenty of open parkland, and a good restaurant. The nearby towns of Krugersdorp and Rustenburg also had nature reserves, and the latter was also famous for its "Kloof", a massive cleft in the rocky hillside. These two parks were not stocked with the range of exotic animals as were their larger cousins, but they did contain various species of buck and even some giraffe. We were thus never stuck for somewhere to go for a day, in order to enjoy the sights and sunshine of this country.

When people think of game parks in South Africa, the one that will spring to mind most often is probably the Kruger. This was the nation's first animal reserve, being established in 1898 by the President after whom it is named. It is one of the largest of its kind in the world, measuring about 220 miles long and 40 miles wide—a similar area to that of Wales. The park is located 252 miles to the east of Johannesburg, against the Mozambique border, and with what is now Zimbabwe to the north. There are several entrance gates along the fenced perimeter. Once inside, a network of roads traverse the park, most with a strict speed limit of 25 miles per hour. There are several secure rest camps, the gates of which are closed at nights for obvious safety reasons. Only at these locations, plus a few hides and picnic areas, are visitors permitted to leave their vehicles.

In September, 1976 we made the first of several visits to this park, keen to see nature in the raw. Today, there are many private reserves adjoining the Kruger, offering expensive luxury accommodation. Very few of these existed in our day but, in any event, financial constraints pointed us toward much more modest lodgings. These were the "Rondavels" in the rest camps, provided by the National Parks Board. They were quite basic—we still jokingly use the term "Ordinary Huts", taken from the official park regulations, to describe hotel rooms. They were nevertheless quite acceptable, with the main ablutions being in a communal block. All the camps had decent restaurants, so residents did not need to bring their own food for the main meals.

The atmosphere in the park at nights was quite magical. Strange animal noises could often be heard coming from the surrounding bush, but it was reassuring to know we were protected by locked gates. Apparently this was not the case in the early days, when there were no perimeter fences around these camps. Rondavel doors were provided with a spy hole to check for marauding lion and other dangerous creatures, before venturing outside. Up above the stars shone brightly, with the constellation of the Southern Cross prominent in the sky. On one occasion it was so clear that we could even see the Clouds of Magellan, small patches that are satellite galaxies of our own Milky Way.

Contrary to what people might think, game viewing was very much a case of pot luck. Cars could only drive along the tracks from dawn until dusk. Some days you were lucky to see even a few buck; on other occasions lion or elephant would be right by the roadside. Animals could be in the thick bush, just a few yards away, but were well camouflaged and could not be seen. The locals advised us that winter was the best time for viewing. During this season the foliage would be less dense after the deciduous trees had lost their leaves, and one could then see further.

Patience and a keen eye were constantly needed, and the visitor just had to accept the hours, or even days, when the viewing

The Animals

revealed little of interest. The park was not being deliberately stocked with game for the tourists' benefit, but was an area that naturally sustained a certain amount of animal life. By contrast, it was rumored that the luxury, private camps were so deliberately over-stocked with animals that good viewing was virtually guaranteed. We preferred to be where nature was left to its own devices.

Our photo album reminds us that we were very lucky with the game viewing on our first visit to the Kruger. We saw hippo wallowing in a pool, elephant quite close to the road, zebra, giraffe, gnu, buck, and baboons. The highlight was a rare sighting of one of the big cats. The cars in front of us were backed up, and many had stopped. Nothing of note was obvious, but then another motorist shouting across, told us, "There's a leopard up a tree, complete with its kill of a small deer." Despite the rule against leaving the safety of one's car, some twit had to throw caution to the wind, and risk standing outside to try and photograph the animal through a zoom lens. That person was me! Fortunately, there was no official there to issue a fine on that occasion—and the leopard was not yet ready to look on me as its next meal.

We took two more holidays in the Kruger Park, in addition to visiting on day permits when staying at locations close to one of the gates. There was a particularly memorable sighting one day when we were driving along. One of the boys suddenly shouted out excitedly, "Look Dad, straight ahead; look, look!" A large elephant had just emerged from the bush, only about 25 yards in front of our car. The animal turned to face us, and trumpeted loudly. It was prudent to start reversing the vehicle, ready to take some sort of evasive action should the massive creature move in our direction.

What then happened was quite captivating. Having established its authority, and determined there was no threat, the matriarch elephant calmly led its small family—out of sight until this moment—across the road and into the bush on the other side. Such events are surely worth the hours of driving through the park with little to see.

Lion were not in abundance, and we only once saw one. It appeared to be an old male, and it was walking calmly by the side of the road and past the row of cars that had stopped to take a closer look. Contrary to popular belief, lion are not the most dangerous animals for humans; more people are killed by hippopotami, buffalo and crocodile. On another day, my flouting of the rules by half stepping out of the car to take a photograph brought its just punishment. A traffic policeman—not a park ranger as one might have expected—gave me a ticket for this offence. It seemed a tad hypocritical that he, himself, was freely walking around in the open air, ready to pounce on any law-breaker. Like all the police, including the traffic cops, he carried a pistol in a buttoned-up holster, but this would not have been much defense against a pride of hungry lion. Nevertheless, his chances would no doubt have been better than mine.

One snag with this "stay in the vehicle" rule was, what to do if one's car breaks down? This happened to us twice. On the first occasion we were driving along, having just left a rest camp, when the engine just stopped. All efforts to re-start it failed. Mild panic set in. What do we do now? This was a time before mobile telephones. We asked a passing motorist if he would please drive back into the camp and report this to an official. Eventually, to our relief, a breakdown truck appeared and towed us back into the safety of the camp. In order to connect the tow-rope, the mechanic obviously had to leave his vehicle, but this did not seem to concern him.

The second occasion was even more worrying for us. We then had three children, and had to bring with us all the equipment needed for a holiday in the park. To enable us to accommodate all this stuff, and to be able to spread out in comfort, we had hired a people carrier. Unfortunately, the vehicle turned out to be so decrepit that it kept breaking down. Having to try and push-start this conveyance in the middle of a game reserve was not particularly amusing, but fortunately we survived.

Game viewing was by no means restricted to the Kruger Park; some of the other reserves have already been mentioned in earlier chapters, and we visited most of the remaining ones during our 20 years. Three were provincial game parks in Kwazulu, which is part of the Natal: Hluhluweo, Imfolozi, and Umkhuze. These names are from the Zulu language, and it took us some time before we could pronounce them anything near correctly. Whilst not stocked with a variety of animals to rival their famous neighbor, these were in very beautiful surroundings, and they also had accommodation. We added several good sightings of white rhino to our tally of wildlife seen, and even a distant view of its elusive black cousin.

The Addo Elephant Park, near Port Elizabeth in the Eastern Cape area, was established in 1931 for the conservation of these noble pachyderms. Our single visit there was not very productive, only yielding a rather distant sighting from a raised viewing platform. The country also contained more than one crocodile farm, but we were somewhat surprised to learn that these were not established to protect the animals, but to produce the leather for expensive fashions, and meat for specialist restaurants. In some parts of South Africa, various wild animals just roamed freely. The Cape Point Nature Reserve is unfenced, and is noted for its baboons that jump onto the car and try to drink from the windscreen washer jets. We were warned that it was not advisable to try and interact with these creatures, due to their big teeth and potential aggression.

Walking trails added another dimension to wildlife viewing for the enthusiast, and allowed a person to really feel at one with nature, even though these usually excluded dangerous animals. On one of these walks, a ranger led us across the open veldt to a clump of trees. After being warned to stay very quiet, he pointed to a pair of white rhino no more than about 50 yards away. Whilst this may have seemed a very threatening situation for unarmed people on foot, it was the animals that ran away when they saw us. At another location, the ranger pointed to a wide burrow that had been dug in the ground. He told us to stand well back, and then rolled a small stone down the hole. In a flash, about six wart hogs came hurtling out of the burrow, brushing past us and shrieking as they ran away. This was more frightening for us than the close encounter with the rhino!

By far the most endearing of these "back to nature" experiences was our stay at a location called Maduma Bona, not too far away from the Kruger Park. Each guest was allocated a well-appointed chalet out of sight of any other building, in its own grounds that included a small outdoor swimming pool. Guests could walk around the whole park unaccompanied, and perhaps see some Impala buck, giraffe or other "safe" animals. The most delightful treat was in store for us on our first morning.

Through the fence came a small family of warthog. We remembered our previous encounter with these creatures, when they noisily ran away, and we quickly closed the door in case they were aggressive. We need not have worried, as they were just doing their rounds, seeing what scraps of food they could scavenge. Once reassured, we offered them a few left-overs, and one animal even came into the house and let us pet it. This was a daily occurrence to which we looked forward, and the whole holiday was a most memorable experience. It was as if a little bit of heaven had come down to earth.

Chapter 10

The Places

SOUTH AFRICA HAS MORE memorable sights to offer than just the wildlife, and there are many places of natural beauty and spectacular scenery to visit. Full details of these can be found in the many travel guides available, but the present narrative is not intended to be one of them. Instead, its aim is to share just a few of the occasions when what we saw resulted in a spontaneous "wow"!

Whilst some countries are famous for their impressive buildings, the outcome of nature's handiwork often turns out to be the most awe inspiring. Table Mountain was nominated earlier in this book as probably the most outstanding example seen, but some others in our adopted country were not far behind.

Several amazing views resulted from the dramatic drop in elevation from the 6,000 feet of the Highveld, where we lived, to about 2,000 feet at the town of Nelspruit, just over 200 miles to the east. When travelling in this direction, much of the drop occurs on an escarpment over a relatively short distance. At certain points, where the fall is particularly steep, people can look down on the land below as if from an airplane. Our first taste of this was along part of the main road known as "Long Tom Pass". We pulled into a lay-by, conveniently situated at a good viewing point, to take photographs and gaze at the series of gently rolling hills falling away below us. The closest ones were a light purple color in the bright sunshine. As they receded into the distance, the color then changed to turquoise, and then to a dark, misty green.

As we drank in this panorama of nature's handiwork at its best, some African ladies suddenly appeared over the barrier at the side of the road, and offered soapstone carvings for sale. Just a short distance down the slope we could see other women carving and polishing the pieces of stone. The group clearly knew where the tourists were most likely to stop. Of course, we had to buy something, and the stone really does feel as if you are holding a piece of soap.

Continuing the journey eastwards, there is an even more spectacular view, but it requires a detour on minor roads, and is thus likely to be missed by the uninformed visitor. It has the inspirational name of "God's Window", and we were told that visitors could stand right on the edge of the Highveld and look down. This sounded rather dangerous; a fall of 4,000 feet without a parachute is not something to relish, but we could not resist including this in our itinerary.

After parking the car, we carefully made our way through a small area of woodland and soon arrived at the viewing point. Once there, we need not have worried too much about the safety aspect. Yes, the level ground came to a sudden end, and there was no fence or other barrier to stop people going any further. In front of us, the downward slope was exceedingly steep, but it was not quite as frightening as standing on the edge of a vertical cliff and gazing out to sea. Nevertheless, it certainly did give the feeling of looking down on the world from a privileged vantage point.

To capture this vista required a skilled landscape artist, who knew how to represent on canvass the sight that opened up before us; photographs certainly can not do it justice. Thick pine forests were laid out beneath us, which were interspersed with other patches of trees and grasslands. After this, the undulating land just seemed to go on for ever, with each successive layer becoming ever paler and fainter. In the middle distance, a single plume of smoke lazily spiraling into the sky indicated that there must have been some people living and working on this part of the escarpment.

Despite careful searching, however, we could see no other sign of habitation.

Continuing a little further to the east, there is the Blyde River Canyon. This is one of the world's largest examples of its kind, and probably the biggest that is clothed in green foliage. The gorge is about 16 miles long, and nearly 2,500 feet deep in places. It was mostly carved out by the river from which it takes its name, which drops approximately 4,000 feet during its passage through the mountains. Erosion has also played a part. It has carved out many rocky hillocks and outcrops, three of which look remarkably like round buildings with sloping roofs, standing close together. Perhaps not surprisingly, they are named: "The Three Rondavels". The many hills, ledges and steps break up what would otherwise just be a uniform, winding valley, so the eye does not become bored when feasting on this unique creation of nature.

Very different is the Fish River Canyon in what is now Namibia (see chapter 8). This is the largest such geographical feature in Africa, but it is virtually devoid of vegetation. It looks very stark and barren, with a uniformly brown color. In the strong sunlight a person could be forgiven for thinking that it is an alien landscape. Indeed, "Buzz" Aldrin's description of the moon during the first landing there in 1969 could equally apply here: "Magnificent desolation!" The contrast between this and its Blyde River cousin could not be greater. In a struggle to create an equally concise epithet that does justice to this great, green, undulating valley, the best attempt so far is: "Verdantly awesome!"

During our visit there we stopped at an ideal picnic spot where we could continue to enjoy the view. Not content with just bringing along a cold, packed lunch and a thermos flask, we owned a spirit stove so we could heat up some food or drink. After placing the device on a suitable spot on the ground, the burner was lit. Calamity followed, as somehow the grass around the stove also caught fire and seemed to be spreading faster than we could stamp it out. Fortunately, we eventually managed to extinguish the flames, and hoped that we had not alarmed the other visitors who were dotted around. We could just picture the newspaper headline: "British tourists set fire to the Blyde River canyon!"

Although formed by human hand, and so not strictly "natural", another attraction that cannot be omitted from any tourist's "to do" list is the Kimberly "Big Hole". Following the discovery of diamonds on the surface, digging started there in the year 1871 and continued until 1914. At its peak, it was worked by 50,000 miners and, in total, yielded about 3,000 kilograms (14 and a half million carats) of diamonds. Old photographs indicate that this was a very hazardous operation, and many died from accidents and disease. The plot was divided into numerous small squares, and each team of miners just excavated their own claim, using a rope and pulley system to convey the spoils to the surface. As can be imagined, the groups worked at different speeds, and this resulted in big differences in height between these tiny pieces of land. Collapsing of unsupported plots must have been commonplace, sometimes with disastrous consequences.

By the time the mine was exhausted, the hole measured some 1,500 yards in diameter. This is large enough to swallow a small town of 360 houses. It is nearly 2,370 feet deep but, over the years, debris and water have reduced the depth somewhat. Standing on the viewing platform at the side of this gaping pit half filled with green water, it is easy to struggle for suitable superlatives to describe what one sees—it is just big, big, BIG! Houses on the other side of the hole are like match boxes in the distance. The current site owners have done an excellent job in re-constructing the original little mining village next to the hole. The buildings are largely of corrugated iron, and are complete with waxwork figures and music to add to the authenticity. It is well worth a visit.

The Augrabies Falls are situated about 75 miles to the west of the town of Uppington, which is the last sign of civilization before reaching the southern entrance to what was then South West Africa. Whilst not being one of the biggest waterfalls in the world, they are regarded as the largest over granite rocks. One of the two major rivers in the country, the Orange, divides into several channels before cascading 200 feet down into the gorge below, which is itself 800 feet deep.

When, along with Peter, the two of us made a detour to visit the falls during our journey to South West Africa (see chapter 8), we clambered over the grey, slate-colored rocks to obtain the best view. A lazy lizard was sunbathing on one of the stones, and did not seem to mind the two of us encroaching on its territory. Like the Fish River Canyon, there is no vegetation but, as the guidebook states, with its distinctive rushing sound, this makes for a spectacular listening, as well as viewing, experience.

Our aim to try and visit every town, and see every notable sight, in South Africa was largely accomplished during our 20 years, partly through business trips but also during family holidays. This even included the tiny town Pofadder in the Northern Cape, one of the most remote settlements in the country, to which parents sometimes threaten to send their naughty children if they didn't behave. We just had to pose and take a photograph next to the road sign showing the town's name, to prove to skeptical friends that we had indeed been there!

Among the other memories that spring to mind are the fascinating Baobabs, sometimes known as the "upside-down tree". This is just what they look like. The silver-grey trunks are so massive that they withstand the force of elephants rubbing up against them. Small, root-like branches perch on the tops of these trees, which are covered in green leaves during the growing season. They exist mostly in the north and east of the country, and are sufficiently rare to become tourist attractions. The trees can live for several thousand years and they certainly do have a prehistoric look about them.

Even rarer is the 1,000-year-old Wonderboom ("Tree of Wonder"), a variety of fig, just north of Pretoria—this is the only such specimen in the world. It is unique because the drooping branches have taken root to form a grove of 13 daughter trunks around the parent tree. The leaves are not like those of the more familiar turkey fig trees, which have a stubby-finger appearance. Instead, they are pointed and shiny with no indentations.

A tree famous for a completely different reason is the "Hanging Tree" at Griquatown, visited with David when the two of us toured the more remote regions of the Northern Cape. In the early part of the 1800's this area became a centre for stock thieves and other outlaws, who were suitably dealt with on the horizontal bough provided by nature as a convenient scaffold. The tree is now in a resident's private garden, but he very kindly let us in to have a look, and to photograph it. One part of the tree, now massive, had separated from the main trunk and was growing at an angle of about 45 degrees. At about 10 feet from the ground, a thick bough branched off this, and it was indeed perfectly horizontal. There must have been a problem with damage or disease at some time, because the branch has been foreshortened so that only approximately three feet now remains. If trees could talk, this one would surely have some gruesome tales to tell.

Also in this region, on a hillside just outside a small town called Kakamas, are the graves of six German soldiers, the only ones to be killed on South African soil during World War 1. The site is close to the border of South West Africa, which at that time was a German protectorate. In 1915 there was a skirmish on the South African side, and troops from both forces were killed. The graves look down on the semi-desert of the Karoo, with some cultivated land in the distance. It is a poignant reminder of the Great War, and the immense loss of life on both sides.

The list of notable places visited and things seen could go on for much longer, but it will end here with the response to a question many people have asked: "Did you have any trouble with snakes?" In fact we saw very few during our 20 years. In addition to the harmless varieties, seen on a couple of occasions, the common venomous species include the Rinkhals (a variety of cobra), Boomslang (Tree Snake), and Puff Adder. On our visits to the game parks, we saw a Rinkhals gracefully moving along the grass nearby, which raised its head when the car horn was mischievously tooted. On another occasion, there was one on a dirt road that had recently been run over, but the poor thing was still alive.

One morning back home in Benoni, when taking our dog for a walk to the nearby lake, something that looked like a log on a rock caught my eye. The dog went close to investigate, but the "log" suddenly reared up—it was a Rinkhals! My frantic scream of: "Sandy, come here" must have awakened the neighborhood. Fortunately, the dog dutifully obeyed, and the snake then slithered off toward the lake.

When I mentioned this incident to other local residents, the response was, "Oh yes, didn't you know? They live in the swampy land next to the lake, and feed on the frogs that breed there." This area was a popular recreation spot, and every weekend there were families having barbeques, and children playing by the waterside. Nobody seemed to worry, and the snakes were probably more fearful of the people than the people were of them. Thus, to answer the question: "Did we have any trouble with snakes?"

"No, but they were not far away, and there was a close encounter that could have turned nasty."

Chapter 11

Further Reflections

In August, 1976, we again paused to reflect on our experiences and record another tape. It is interesting to identify what newcomers to a country may see as novel, but that local residents regard as commonplace.

One of the first things we noticed in all the towns, and especially Johannesburg, was the large number of traders selling fruit and vegetables on the street. The produce was sold by the bowlful, at a standard price that seemed very cheap, and was obviously intended for people who could only afford enough food for that day. Although selling by volume rather than weight is now regularly seen on market stalls in the UK, perhaps to avoid confusing the buyers when the metric system was introduced, this was not the case when we emigrated. We thought this was an excellent idea, especially for those on a limited budget, as you could see exactly what you were buying.

Two other novel practices caught our attention. The first was African ladies carrying loads on their heads, without having to hold on to the package. Although pictures of this had been seen before, we did not anticipate how routine it would be, especially in the middle of busy towns. One of the girls at the biscuit factory told me later that mothers taught their daughters this skill from an early age. It was very graceful and good for the deportment, as the women had to remain upright and steady at all times. A useful ability if they could master it, but our family's attempts to even keep a book on our heads whilst walking inevitably led to disaster.

The second of these early observations also involved African ladies; this time it was the way they carried their babies, or even toddlers, on their backs. The infants were held by a shawl, as if they were sitting in a hammock with their legs dangling out, and the women then tied this in front of their waists and chests. We later learned that children sometimes spent the whole of their day like this, whilst their mothers went about their daily tasks, or even their paid work. It all seemed so natural, and the women probably hardly knew their babies were there for most of the time. There were clearly many advantages in this, including that the youngsters were constantly kept warm, safe, and stimulated. Their mothers did not have to worry about where their children were, and it saved the cost of paying for a childminder.

Sadly, we did not have to go far to see evidence of poverty. There were beggars on the streets, and people were sleeping rough in doorways, particularly in Johannesburg. No welfare state or social security existed in South Africa at that time, although some medical provision was made for impoverished black people—in segregated hospitals. Those who were in employment paid into medical insurance schemes, with the company also contributing. There were, however, limits to what could be claimed in different categories, such as prescriptions, doctor's visits, and operations.

Whilst we found that this normally covered all our medical expenses, those who had serious accidents or required extensive treatment and hospitalization, could rapidly exceed the maximum allowances and accumulate very large debts. There was no state pension, but working people could subscribe to one of the private schemes, again with contributions from the employer.

We very quickly learned that petrol stations closed at midday on Saturdays and only opened again on Monday mornings. This regulation was introduced to save fuel, at a time when there was a world-wide oil shortage, and economic sanctions were operating against South Africa. Weekend travelling was thus restricted to how far you could drive on one tank of fuel. There was also a strict limit on how much petrol could be carried or stored in a can.

Distances between major towns in South Africa are long, but energetic people in the Johannesburg area thought nothing of driving over 300 miles to the nearest coastal resort of Durban for the weekend. Not all cars could even make the journey one-way without filling up, and there was an added complication. Because of the altitude differential, engines in most cars on the Highveld were tuned to use a lower octane grade of petrol than were those driven at sea level. On the journey to Durban, it was usual to stop half way there and fill up with higher octane fuel. On the return journey, motorists stopped to refuel with the lower rating.

It was therefore important to plan a journey carefully. We were only caught out once on a Sunday, but managed to scrounge (illegally!) a small amount of petrol from the proprietor of the guesthouse at which we were staying, to help us on our way.

Something that we did not think about before emigrating, was that Christmas in South Africa falls in the middle of summer. Many businesses closed down from the 15th of December for a month, when all but essential personnel were obliged to take their entire year's holiday allowance. Although this provided a nice long break, working non-stop for the remaining 11 months, except for bank holidays, led to a noticeable fall in efficiency as the shutdown period grew closer. One advantage of this arrangement was that iterant workers had the time to return to their homelands for Christmas, complete with an annual bonus in their pockets. It was common practice for all levels of staff to receive such a payment, which usually amounted to a double check—less a large chunk of tax.

We had now been in our own house in Benoni for five months. The process of buying the property entailed battling the Afrikaner bureaucracy, as mentioned in our earlier reflections (chapter 7). Completing the formalities for the rates, electricity service, water supply, and other municipal requirements was a long and frustrating process. After paying the solicitor's account relating to our house purchase, he then sent a second bill for something he had previously forgotten. Shortly thereafter, he sent yet a further demand for another omission. My protestations fell on deaf ears, even when taken to the level of not paying his last bill and waiting for the summons to appear in court. Before the case was heard, the Afrikaans magistrate said that there was no chance of me winning. There was no alternative but to pay up, which I did—in installments, taking as long as possible.

The house was an older dwelling, with a corrugated iron roof. Whilst this might seem more appropriate for a shanty town, it was quite typical of many of the more modestly-priced properties in South Africa. The fact that our neighbors in similar houses included a retired teacher, a doctor, and a minister of the church, confirms that they were quite acceptable to middle-class professionals. Not only was the roof metal, but so also were the window frames, and the ceilings were made from pressed tinplate embossed with a range of patterns. The gardens were of reasonable size, with a small orchard at the back but no swimming pool. Our house had the usual servant's room attached to the back of the garage, but we used this only for storage. The only problem was the typical one of lack of insulation against the cold winters; only when we bought a solid-fuel-burning stove could we keep warm.

The boys were by now settled at their school in Benoni. The starting age for education in South Africa was later than that in the UK. Depending on the birthday date, a child could be as old as seven before going to school. In common with others in our home country, each of our boys had begun their education by the age of five. Knowing that they had already completed some years of schooling, when they enrolled at their first school in Springs the principal allocated them to classes with children older than themselves. This, plus the differences in culture and teaching style, did not make for a happy start for the poor lads, especially David who was only aged six at the time. After a week or so, we managed to persuade the school principal to transfer him to the previous year's class, and this helped him acclimatize.

We asked our two sons to record their thoughts on the best and worst things about life in this new country. David's response was, "We start school at eight o'clock in the morning, but finish at half past one. This means I can take the dog for a walk in the afternoons, and go to the shop for sweets. The best thing is the long summer, with a shorter winter without rain. The worst is being bossed around by the Afrikaners, but Peter fell off his bike and an Afrikaner helped him."

Peter, who was then aged 10, commented, "The best thing I have seen is the acrobatic dancing at the mine dance. The sun is good, and I like to swim in the outdoor pools. I like being at home during the afternoons. Our dog Sandy had pups. The worst thing is having to learn Afrikaans at school."

We were pleased that these comments indicated the boys had settled into their new lives, although it was unfortunate that they were expressing some anti-Afrikaans sentiments. What would not have been evident to most non-South Africans was that, although there were obvious cultural differences between blacks and whites, so also were there such differences between the two white "races". As has already been mentioned, my own experiences had led to frustration with Afrikaner bureaucracy, officiousness and inefficiency. Sometimes the officials we had to deal with appeared to be deliberately unhelpful, manifesting a superior attitude that seemed to say, "We are the ones who make the decisions."

We wondered if there was a particular reason for this attitude. Was there some resentment against British people and, if so, why? It might help to try and look at this from the point of view of the local residents. The Afrikaners were proud of their pioneering work, and the sacrifices they had made in opening up this country. But they still retained all the power, and were not taking any obvious steps toward a full democracy. Because of this, economic sanctions had been imposed on them by many countries, including Britain. In order to maintain and develop manufacturing and technology, immigrants with the necessary skills and experience were needed, hence the incentive of the assisted-passage scheme of which we had taken full advantage. It must have been quite galling for residents to have to welcome immigrants from the very countries that were also opposing them.

Further Reflections

The best way to handle this, we realized, was to try and become fully integrated into the life and culture of South Africa whilst we were there. This included supporting the national sports teams, being enthusiastic about what the country had to offer, and helping rather than criticizing. There were many small ways that a person could try and influence situations that were morally unacceptable, without falling foul of the authorities. Most of all, it was important not to follow the example of the Rhodesian immigrants, by adopting a "when we" attitude, as mentioned in chapter 4. In sum, we had to behave as honorary South African citizens whilst we were there. In our everyday interactions, we found many individuals whose first language was Afrikaans to be kind and helpful, and we made lasting friendships that remain to this day.

Listening to our recordings again, many years later, it did seem that we were quickly succumbing to the sin of cultural stereotyping and prejudice. Maybe this was so rife in South Africa, and especially with the black-white dichotomy, that typecasting quickly became automatic. We could understand the reservations our sons had in having to learn Afrikaans, a language not spoken in any other country, and one that would forever be linked with an oppressive regime. It was nevertheless not conducive to harmonious relationships to assume that every Afrikaner was a bad person, and someone to be avoided. The fact that David, who was then only seven years old, had felt the need to highlight that it was an Afrikaner who had helped Peter after his bicycle accident, shows just how early in life such typecasting can occur.

Perhaps a word of explanation is due concerning our dog, Sandy, who was mentioned for the first time in the comments from both the boys. Shortly before we moved from our house at Springs, we were visited by this female canine. She seemed to be hungry, so we threw her a lump of bread, which was instantly gobbled down. Thinking she would then go away, we ignored her, but she did not ignore us. The dog was still there the next day, so we telephoned the local animal welfare organization and asked if they would come and take her in. Rather craftily, the person on the other end of the line suggested that we should look after the animal for a few days, and call again later if we still had a problem. There could only have been one outcome: we adopted the dog, and called her Sandy because of her color.

We subsequently heard that somebody who lived in the area had abandoned this dog. Her given name was Cindy which, to the dog, would have sounded very similar to Sandy, so it is not surprising that she responded to this. It was a common practice in South Africa to have at least one dog, as they were very good at barking at prowlers and discouraging them from doing any mischief. Sandy thus became our faithful companion for many years.

Not long after we moved to Benoni, there was a commotion going on outside the house one morning. On investigating, we found Sandy somewhat reluctantly in flagrante with the ugliest male dog in the neighborhood. Despite me chasing the suitor off, the damage was obviously already done, because about 12 weeks later, there was the patter of many tiny feet. Hence Peter's comments on the recording about the pups.

Two months before we made this tape, there had been a serious confrontation between blacks and whites, which had far-reaching consequences for South Africa. This became known as the "Soweto Riots". All we heard at the time was that there had been unrest and violence in the black township of Soweto, near Johannesburg. This was the largest such conurbation in the country, and its name was a condensation of the phrase "South West Township." Although we lived far enough to the east to be clear of these events, we were warned that the roads leading in and out of the trouble spots were dangerous, and must be avoided.

It was only later that the true story emerged. The government had earlier issued an "Afrikaans Medium Decree", which stated that half the subjects in black schools had to be taught in Afrikaans. Whilst all school pupils had to learn both of the official languages, the new requirement to also teach other subjects in a tongue associated with the apartheid regime, was clearly unacceptable. Such a requirement did not apply to schools for white children.

There had already been resistance to this ruling in some townships. A student representative group in Soweto planned a peaceful protest march for 16th of June, 1976. Thousands of high school pupils took to the streets, but they found their way blocked by the police. Although the protestors did not pose a physical threat, they were fired upon by the police. The violence escalated over the next day or two, and at least 176 rioters were killed, possibly many more, plus a large number of others were injured.

Although the situation did stabilize after a few days, and the decree was rescinded, the police action was severely condemned by many, both within South Africa and abroad. Much damage was done to the country's reputation, as well as its economic stability. The events surrounding the Soweto Riots started a chain-reaction of resistance, along with demands for change made by moderate South Africans as well as the international community. The national government could not ignore these, and some improvements were slowly introduced. Ultimately, but only after a further 18 years, this resulted in the first democratic elections (see chapter 17).

Chapter 12

The Law, Guns, and Danger

AS MIGHT BE EXPECTED from the multi-national history of South Africa, the legal system is commensurately hybrid. The main influences are a civil law system that came from the Dutch, a common law structure inherited from the British, and a customary law procedure that originated from the indigenous African population. The range of law courts is similar to that in the UK, namely: magistrates, high court, and Supreme Court of Appeal. There is also an African court that deals with cases involving traditional customs and tribal matters.

In practice, however, the law does not always operate in a way that might be expected. Our experience suggested that there could be an element of "who you know", and that some decisions seemed to be made with a degree of discretion not covered in the statute book. Whilst this can sometimes work to one's benefit, it can also have the opposite effect. An incident that immediately springs to mind occurred during my drive home from work one afternoon. In order to catch speeding motorists, the traffic police had followed their usual practice of laying rubber strips across the road, which were linked to a device that recorded the vehicle's speed as it drove over them.

No doubt my thoughts were preoccupied with the anticipation of a delicious evening meal, washed down with a glass of the grape. My daydreaming was rudely interrupted when a traffic cop suddenly jumped out of the bushes where he had been hiding, and waved me down. I stopped the car, got out and, fearing the inevitability of a traffic fine, my mind raced with excuses and apologies.

What happened next did not quite fit this anticipated scenario. The officer smiled, shook my hand and said, "Good afternoon, Sir, how are you?" This caught me off guard. He continued, "Our meter indicates you were driving 10 kph over the speed limit. Do you agree with this?" Of course, there was no point in me denying it. "Then I am afraid I shall have to give you this Speeding Ticket", he said, noting down all the pertinent details. After a few more pleasantries, he wished me a nice day, and waved me off to complete my journey home without a trace of anger or resentment in my mind.

The officer's manner impressed me greatly. Here was a man doing a job that would usually make his victims very cross. Instead, like me, they probably went on their ways (cautiously!) with a smile on their faces. It seemed appropriate to write to his station commander, commending him for the way he was carrying out his duties. A few days after having done this, a call came through on my work telephone. "Mister Lowis, the station commander here. Thank you very much for your letter. The speeding charge will be dropped."

After taking a few moments for this to sink in, my response was, "This is very kind of you, but I do admit to driving over the speed limit."

"That's all right", he replied. "But no charges will be made against you."

This was certainly not my intention, but only to give credit where it was due. Whilst this ended well for me on that occasion, it did indicate a degree of freedom that law enforcement officers used, without rigidly following procedures. Whether or not this was technically permissible was another matter.

On another occasion, whilst walking along a main street in Benoni, right in front of me a pickpocket lifted a purse that a woman had carelessly left on top of the contents of her shopping basket. Having witnessed this, my reaction was to grab the villain (fortunately a man smaller than me) in an arm lock, and shout to the woman that she had been robbed. The pickpocket immediately dropped the purse on the ground, but the woman then grabbed it. "Go into the shop and ask the assistant to telephone the police", I said to her, whilst keeping a firm hold on the man. But the shopkeeper declined to become involved, and the woman just muttered something and walked off.

My Good Samaritan deed had left me standing in the street holding a bloke in an arm lock, trying to otherwise look inconspicuous. There were many curious glances from the passing shoppers, but nobody offered to help. What does a person do in such a situation, I asked myself?

After a minute or two, a man stopped and asked me what was going on. When he had heard the story, he shouted at the pickpocket in Afrikaans, and slapped him across the face. He then told me that he was a special constable, and that it was not worth calling the police because the other witnesses, including the victim, had now disappeared. He suggested that I let the man go, as he had just given him a verbal warning about what would happen if he was caught again. With feelings of relief, coupled with some disappointment that my heroic efforts had not resulted in a criminal being locked up, I duly released the culprit from the arm lock. He quickly melted into the crowds, which was no doubt what he was adept at doing.

Whilst this might have seemed to be a case of justice not being done, in retrospect such discretionary judgments meted out by those who knew the system, may have been the best practical way of dealing with situations like this.

An incident that did lead to a court appearance as a witness all started when a chap came to my house one evening, to look at a bicycle that I had advertised for sale. A moment after the visitor left to return to his car, which was parked right outside, he rushed back and said, "My car radio has just been stolen; help me to see if we can find the thief—he can't have gone far."

"All right", I replied. "You drive round the block one way, and I'll go in the opposite direction." Only a short time into my circuit,

The Law, Guns, and Danger

a man walked past the front of my car, carrying something like a box that had a wire hanging from it. "Hey you!" I shouted, from the safety of my vehicle. "You've just stolen a car radio." The man then calmly put his package down in some bushes near the path, and started to walk away.

At that moment, my colleague drove up, and was quickly briefed on what had happened. Once he had heard my story, he jumped out of his car, chased after the culprit, and led him back to the bushes. Sure enough, his radio was there.

My visitor then locked the thief in the back of his car, and we telephoned the police. Minutes passed, but there was no response. After a second call without any action, my companion said that he would drive to the police station in town, and personally hand the captive over to the authorities. Although the reluctant passenger was of slight build, and seemed quite docile now, this seemed to me to be a risky thing to do. Despite my concern, and offer to help, he said that there was no need for me to accompany him, and assured me there would be no trouble. He then got into his car, and drove off.

The main point of this story concerns the subsequent trial at the magistrate's court, about a week later, when my presence was demanded as a witness. After presenting my version of the event, the magistrate asked me, "Can you identify the person you saw hiding the radio in the bushes?"

My response was, "No, it was at night, and I can't remember exactly what he looked like."

A look of exasperation, or maybe even mild panic, appeared on the face of the magistrate. "Look around the courtroom", he said. "See if there is anyone you think *might* be the culprit."

Now there was only one person in the room who was not white, and he was the man in the dock. My recollection was that the thief was dark-skinned so, pointing to the prisoner, I said, "He mostly resembles that man, but . . . "

Before my sentence could be completed, which would have emphasized that this did not amount to a positive identification, the magistrate interrupted and announced to all present, "Let the record show that the witness has identified the accused. The witness may now step down."

Fortunately for the justice system, the victim of the robbery told me later that the accused was indeed the man he had taken into custody, and that the thief already had a criminal record. He had now been given a custodial sentence. Thus, there had been no miscarriage of justice. Notwithstanding the satisfactory outcome on this occasion, this still left me with an uncomfortable feeling that people may be found guilty on flimsy evidence. If the radio thief had been represented by a sharp lawyer, he or she would certainly have challenged my rather doubtful identification of his client as the culprit.

Two memorable incidents occurred at my final place of work, both relating to the same event. This was during our final year in South Africa, and about 12 months after the first democratic elections in 1994, which will be the subject of a later chapter. The political situation was rapidly changing, and the black Africans were emerging from their long struggle against apartheid. It was fully understandable that the frustration now relieved should sometimes express itself on the shop floor, through rebellious behavior toward white staff in senior positions.

The company manufactured a wide range of plastics goods, and was wholly owned by the founder. There were about 125 operatives, and a very lean management team comprising just a production manager, and myself covering both human resources and quality control. Two office staff and a buying clerk completed the list of salaried employees. No time was wasted with management meetings, and all major decisions were taken by the owner.

Trades unions were now permitted, and it had been my job to negotiate a disciplinary procedure with the organization to which most operatives belonged. This included issuing written warnings for misdemeanors, and dismissal if the behavior continued. For a reason now forgotten, but it might have been a test case engineered by the workers themselves, one man had stopped working, and was just sitting at his machine doing nothing. The owner asked me to issue him a written warning. This was done, but there was no change in his behavior. A final written warning was likewise unproductive. The next step was dismissal, and it was my job to initiate this. The reaction was that the entire workforce downed tools in a show of support for the victim.

The first incident arising from this occurred when I returned to my office, only to find it was crammed with as many operatives as could squeeze in. Not thinking that this posed any serious personal threat, my intention was just to collect my belongings and leave the invaders to their illicit occupation. Once inside, however, the door was slammed shut behind me. It was a hostage situation! One of the workers told me to sit down, and started questioning me about the decision to dismiss the disobedient operative.

The scenario had been observed by the production manager just before the door closed, and he had asked the secretary to telephone the police. After a few minutes, my telephone rang, and one of the office ladies said that the police had arrived, but had then gone away again. After hearing the story, they told her that they would not try to force their way into my office, as it might exacerbate the situation and lead to violence. Thanks very much, I thought, that was a great help! But what to do now?

Eventually, the workers agreed to let me telephone their union head office, to suggest that one of the officials come straight away and try to negotiate a resolution to this situation. Fortunately, the union's premises were only a short distance away. About half an hour later, there was a loud cheering noise coming from the factory, as the official marched toward my office. After he had spoken to them in the vernacular, my captors dispersed, and negotiations then continued with the union representative. The eventual outcome was that the operative did keep his job, and there was some sort of compromise that returned the situation to normal.

Because the workers had carried out an illegal act by constraining a person (me) against his will, the police were asked to consider prosecution. After a less than enthusiastic attempt to interview people on the shop floor, only to find that the workers had made a pact to say absolutely nothing, come what may, the attempt to bring the perpetrators to book fizzled out. It was an effective example of how the strength of solidarity can lead to the weak achieving victory over the strong. For many years, this was the only strategy that the victims of apartheid had over the oppressive government.

The second incident linked to this attempt to dismiss the man who had stopped working, was potentially more serious. It was mentioned in chapter 7 that many people possessed firearms, as a defense against being victims of crimes. It was legal to own a gun in that country, provided one held the appropriate license. The University of Sydney has compiled world-wide statistics on gun policy, which reveal that South Africa ranks 17th out of 178 countries in firearm private ownership. In the year 1994, when the event to be described took place, a total of 3.5 million firearms were owned by 2.4 million individuals. This represented some 8.4 percent of the total population, or nearly half the white members if, as is likely, those with gun licenses were mostly from this sector. In addition to this, the researchers estimated that up to perhaps the same number of illicit firearms also existed.

With so many guns in circulation, the high incidence of violent crime should not come as a surprise. Figures from Cambridge University's Small Arms Survey revealed that, in 1994, there was an average of 66.9 homicides per 100,000 people in South Africa, about 90 percent of them being by firearm. There were also a similar number of attempted murders, along with an even larger incidence of robberies with aggravating circumstances. In this very company, the owner was returning from the bank with the payroll, and was held up at the factory gate by armed robbers. On some occasions, it had been my job to collect the money, so it could easily have been me.

The temptation to own a gun myself could not be resisted for long. This was partly for protection purposes, but also to be able to join a gun club and satisfy my schoolboy yearnings for a hobby that would have been difficult to indulge in back in the UK. As it transpired, this became a very absorbing pastime, trying to develop the skills needed to achieve nationally recognized proficiency grades in various categories. There was also a good social element, and we made many friends through the club. It was reassuring to have a weapon during some of our outings, although the law required that these must always be kept out of sight. Only once was one of my firearms used in anger, and that was to dispatch a rat swimming around our garden pool.

To return to the incident of the operator who sat at his machine but refused to work, the company owner asked his son, who had recently joined the team to learn the business, to take some video footage. The idea was that the man would be asked to recommence working. If he refused, then the film could be used at an industrial tribunal hearing as evidence of disobedience. The few white staff members, including me, were asked to be present when this took place. The outcome was that, not only did the man refuse to cooperate, but other operators also stopped work and started to crowd around us. The owner's son then quietly asked a mechanic, who was one of our little group, "Do you have a gun in your car?" The artisan nodded, went off to collect it, and quickly returned with his firearm concealed.

The stalemate continued, but it gradually dawned on us that we were being closely surrounded by a growing number of very angry workers. There were plenty of potential weapons all around us—iron bars, heavy spanners, and pieces of machinery. If the mechanic had been asked to draw his gun, we would certainly have been in for a fight that could have resulted in serious injury, or even loss of life, for any of us. Fortunately, discretion overcame valor and, spotting an open side entrance to the factory, we gradually maneuvered ourselves toward it. Thankfully, our vulnerable little group emerged into the open air, and left the workforce to its own devices. It did not take much effort to realize just how close we had been to a potential disaster. The political climate in democratic South Africa was indeed changing.

Chapter 13

Work and Play

THE DATE WAS NOVEMBER, 1978, and we had been in the country for three years. By then we were feeling quite established, and it was not a "new" adventure any more. When we decided to emigrate, our plan was to stay only for about this length of time. It thus seemed appropriate to record our thoughts again, believing that this would complete the narrative of this episode of our lives. Whilst fate still had many more experiences in store for us, we certainly did not know that then.

There had been a significant event during the previous year—the birth of our third son, Charles. At that time Peter was aged 12 and David nine. The Afrikaners had a quaint expression for a child that was born some time after the previous one: "Laat lammetjie" (pronounced "lart lumekie"), literally meaning "late lamb". We became so used to this description that we still use it today, when referring to other people's children.

In South Africa, where most medical services were private, family doctors performed more functions than was usually the case in England, and this included delivering babies. So, when the time came, we drove to the local cottage hospital, where the midwife telephoned our general practitioner. It was the small hours of the morning, but the doctor came out, delivered the baby, and then went back home to catch up with his sleep.

Work and Play

We were pleased everything had worked out well so far, despite some ups and downs. Peter was in his final year at junior school, and was looking forward going to high school in the following January, along with several of his friends. When asked about the difference between schooling in South Africa compared with the UK, he repeated something he had said nearly two years previously. He said, "I like the early start and finish in this country, as it leaves most of the afternoon for swimming and being outside." Then he added, "There is not much to watch on TV over here, because it's so poor." One thing he did miss were the more frequent trips to the seaside that we were able to do in England, whereas the 350 miles to Durban was a journey usually reserved for the annual holiday.

David also said that he missed the seaside, but added that the open-air swimming pool was not very warm for much of the year. He agreed that the outdoor activities were enjoyable, and had come to the conclusion that he now preferred South Africa as a place to live.

Fast-forward now another 10 months, when we made what was to be our final audio log. As we had by then seemed to have settled into the life of our adopted country, the thought of making more recordings just did not enter our minds. The tapes were originally intended both as an "aid memoire" of our thoughts, feelings and experiences in a different culture, and as a way of keeping in touch with friends and family back in England. After nearly four years, however, our situation was no longer novel. For all the many new adventures that were still lying in wait for us, it would be photographs and home movies that would stimulate our recall of these.

The boys were asked the same questions about what they like most and least about life in South Africa. By now Peter had been at high school for nearly a year. He was finding it rather boring having to learn German, as well the obligatory Afrikaans, and there were no sports during class time. His previous enthusiasm for an early start to the school day, and a finishing time that left most of the afternoon free, had waned somewhat. Was that because he was now a teen-ager, and appreciated a lie-in in the mornings? He was still enjoying outdoor activities, including being a keen boy scout, camping out at a jamboree, and teaching activities to the cubs. Asked which country he liked best, he commented, "I'm not sure, there are good and bad points with both England and where we are now."

David was approaching his 11th birthday, and had remained quite positive about life in our adopted country. He still liked the early finish to school, so that he could enjoy outdoor activities during the afternoons, and that for most of the year it was warm enough to walk around in tee-shirts and shorts. Like his elder brother, he had joined the boy scouts as a cub, and was working for his proficiency badges.

His comments on the worst thing about South Africa reiterated those he made the previous year. He said, "School is strict, and I don't like having to learn Afrikaans. Also, there is only one television channel, which transmits for just three and a half hours in the evening, split between the two official languages." But he was now less sure of which country he preferred to live in. "If we went back to England, we would gain better TV and more creative schooling, but the weather would be worse." He added, "But it would be nice to have some snow again."

Charles, aged just over two years, said "Ah, big red bus!" Whilst this contributed little to the debate on which country was preferred, it did at least demonstrate his developing linguistic skills, and the ability to identify his toys.

My own view, shared by Susan, was that the food was good, and the local wine plentiful at very affordable prices—in those days, many bottles cost less than the equivalent of one British pound. We could afford to eat out when we wanted to, and also enjoy regular barbeques with friends and neighbors. This al fresco dining was usually a "bring and share" activity, where the host provided the charcoal fire and perhaps a salad, and the guests brought their own food to cook, as well as a bottle. This avoided the entire onus being put on one person, and meant that we could enjoy such socializing more frequently, without elaborate planning and expense. Of course, we could not fail to agree with our boys that the climate was a big "plus", especially when the barbeque was followed by splashing around in the back garden swimming pool.

Because there was relatively less competition in the workplace, the job prospects for appropriately qualified people were superior to those in the UK. There had been little opportunity of advancement for me in England; this was very demotivating, and one of the main reasons for emigrating. In South Africa, provided a person was prepared to work hard and use initiative, promotion prospects and financial advancement were generally good. Junior managers and above were usually provided with a company car, although these were taxed quite heavily. There was also a wider degree of freedom to organize one's job, take decisions, and build a reputation.

The downside to all this was a reduced level of job security, and a "hire and fire" attitude, without recourse to labor laws that gave employees certain rights and protection. Sometimes things happened that appeared to be unethical, both in the way people were treated, and the manner in which business was conducted. This is difficult to understand even now, because the impression was gained as much from intuition as from hard evidence. It just seemed that the transparency in the way things were done was not as we were used to in the UK. As will be related shortly, my own work experience fluctuated wildly between dizzy heights and abysmal depths during our time in South Africa.

One of the greatest benefits that came my way was the willingness of many employers to send key personnel on fact-finding trips abroad. Managing directors were aware of the need to keep pace with technical advancements, and not be left behind because of the sanctions being imposed on the country. If the firms had international contacts in similar lines of business, they often arranged overseas visits for senior members of their staff.

In March 1977, after being at the biscuit factory for over two years, my career advanced significantly as a result of being appointed to a more responsible position with a large pharmaceuticals company. The location was just to the west of Johannesburg, not very far from Soweto where the riots had occurred the previous year. It was partly owned by a large American corporation that had similar plants in many other countries.

After less than a year into this new job, the invitation came to visit the USA head office in Chicago, as well as one of their manufacturing units in the southern part of that country. During my almost five years with this organization, there were several visits to other plants in America, as well as in Israel, Australia, and Ireland. Whilst the latter afforded me the opportunity to make a brief visit to my mother in England on the way back, it also included a potentially life-changing incident that be related in chapter 16. Whilst it lasted, this job can be classified as one of the "dizzy heights" referred to earlier. It was at a senior managerial level, paid a good salary, included an up-market company car, and provided opportunities for overseas travel. What more could a career person want from a job?

Life was good. We had moved to a better house, with a swimming pool in the back garden. Our eldest son, Peter, had not been too happy at his high school, so we moved him to a smaller, private school in Benoni that had an excellent record of academic achievement. It happened to be a Jewish institution, which was happy to accept pupils not of that faith, provided that their parents could afford to pay the fees. At its highest level, my position was General Manager Quality Assurance, and entailed ensuring that the exacting specifications supplied by the American partner were strictly adhered to.

There was also an opportunity to carry out some research on interpersonal relations between the black quality control inspectors and the white production supervisors. This included enacting role-play exercises where the job situations were reversed. The chief executive of the company was suitably impressed, and my success in organizing an inter-departmental choir competition one Christmas received similar approval. Promotion soon followed.

However, as the saying goes, "pride comes before a fall." It was not long after returning from an enjoyable week in Sydney, Australia, as a guest quality auditor with the American team that was carrying out an inspection of the manufacturing facility there. The time was approaching five o'clock in the afternoon, and thoughts were turning toward the journey home and a relaxing evening. The telephone rang; it was the managing director. "Mike, can you please come along to my office." Three minutes later, in his lair, he said, "I want you to go now."

There was a moment of puzzled silence from me, accompanied by a strange icy feeling down my back. "What do you mean 'go now'? I don't understand?" was my mumbled response.

"I want you to take your things and leave, and not come back tomorrow."

Again, silence from me. There had been no hint that this was coming, no previous discussion or warning of any dissatisfaction with my performance. What on earth was the reason for this bombshell? The response to my request for an explanation remained unanswered. No reason was forthcoming, but just a reiteration that my services were being terminated—with immediate effect.

The inevitability of this eventually penetrated my confused brain, but the thought of not even being able to say goodbye to my own staff, many of whom had become good friends, was unbearable. Of course, this was the reason why I had only been sent for at the end of the working day—everybody else would have gone home by now. My plea, "Please, I just have to come in tomorrow morning to say my farewells", must have sounded quite hysterical. The managing director eventually agreed. On stumbling back to my office in a daze, my first thought was to immediately telephone Susan, so that she would be prepared. However, my words would not come out when she answered, but she realized that something bad had happened.

This was truly one of the "abysmal depths", mentioned earlier. Nevertheless, it was not untypical of how things could be done in South Africa. There was no recourse, no appeal, and no arbitration in this situation. The agony dragged on for a few more days, due to me being temporarily sent to another location by the company chief executive, but this chapter of my life quickly came to its inevitable conclusion. It was only some time later that there was any inkling of the reason for the dismissal. A chance meeting with another ex-employee of the pharmaceuticals company revealed that, after the sudden departure, my reputation was as something of a hero.

It appeared that an earlier decision of mine to reject a batch of product, because it did not comply with the quality specifications laid down by the American partners, was contrary to the managing director's wishes. He did not like being opposed, especially when it would incur a financial loss for the company, so he took his revenge out on me. The fact that someone had stood their ground was seen by others as commendable. A few years later, a scandal was linked to this same company. Some babies had died because of an alleged contamination of intravenous infusions supplied by them. This was a terrible tragedy, but maybe also poetic justice.

Whilst being one of the very worst experiences of my life, this was not the only such event to occur whilst working in South Africa. The reasons for leaving four of my seven jobs during the 20 years were not my own. This was definitely not a desirable state of affairs, but it was easy to become resigned to it with time. Maybe the fault was my own lack of understanding of how to survive in a labor market different from that in the UK. There were no unemployment payments in South Africa, and it once took me six months to secure another job. Fortunately, Susan was able to do some part-time work for an estate agent. She received good commission from some house sales just at the time when we most needed the money, so we were never in debt.

Looking back at these episodes now, it is clear that we could have been excused for feeling vulnerable and insecure, but somehow life just continued. There was always something about which we could feel positive, always believing that things would work out—which they inevitably did.

To complete this chapter, it might be of interest to comment on the four houses we bought whilst overseas. It has already been mentioned that nearly all domestic dwellings in South Africa were bungalows, on larger plots of land than is typical in England. Most had two bathrooms, before this became more common in the UK. Even with the more modern buildings there was the problem of lack of insulation against the surprisingly cold winter nights. Also, there was the need for every door and window that could be opened to be fitted with burglar bars. Even this did not stop a determined villain breaking in, usually through the roof.

We moved from our first, older tin roof house to a more modern, Spanish-style dwelling when my career was in the ascendancy. When times became more difficult and our finances tighter, we sold this and bought a house that was equally as spacious, but the location was not quite as desirable. This transaction enabled us to put some savings into the bank, and it gave us a degree of financial security. Finally, when our situation could afford it, we upgraded again and bought our final home.

All but the first of our properties had a swimming pool in the back garden. Whilst this might seem a luxury to those living in colder climates, the pools were not without their problems and required continual maintenance. Firstly, the water was circulated through a filter by a pump controlled by a timer. The filter had to be cleaned regularly. There had to be a device for cleaning the bottom of the pool. This could be an automatic suction cleaner, operated through the pump, which crept its way around the pool. Failing this, it had to be done by a hand-held vacuum cleaner.

Leaves had to be constantly scooped up with a net. Every day the chlorine and acidity levels had to be checked, and adjusted with chemicals as required. Despite all this, it was not unusual to look out in the morning and find that the water had turned green. It was only really warm enough to use the pool for three months of the year, but the maintenance had to be continuous. Toward the end of our stay, we decided that having our own pool was hardly worth the effort.

Chapter 14

Customs and Culture

TAKING UP RESIDENCE IN another country not only provides the opportunity to see different landscapes and animals, but also to experience first-hand the beliefs and behavior of a different culture. It is all too easy to fall into the trap of thinking that the way things are done in one's home country, is the only way there is. Living and working with people in other lands not only helps to avoid such insular and parochial attitudes, but it develops a respect for different perspectives. This confirms the old adage: "travel broadens the mind." Also, like any other activity should be, it is enjoyable.

Some aspects have already been discussed, in particular the wonderful natural harmonies of African singing, and the reluctance of individuals to break solidarity with their colleagues, even if it prevents their advancement in the workplace. This chapter will describe a few of the other interesting cultural practices that we experienced during our 20 years.

What we did not expect, in a country that had a modern health service, was the continued belief by many of the indigenous population in witch doctors. Perhaps it would be more correct to use the term "traditional healers", as there were several varieties of these practitioners, although they were often generally referred to as "Sangomas". These roles were open to both men and women, and the healers were consulted not only for mental or physical illness, but also for birth and death rituals, and even for help in finding people or animals that were lost. The treatment may include administering plant or animal medicines, locally referred to as "muti", which the Sangoma had personally made.

There was a philosophy underpinning the work of these people, based on respect for ancestors and a belief in ancestral spirits that may guide and protect the living. Guidance was obtained from the dead by interpreting dreams, throwing the bones, or entering a trance-like state through exhaustive dancing, to allow the ancestor to take possession of the healer's body. Once this state had been achieved, when the healer speaks to his or her patient, it is supposed that it is the voice of the departed.

It would be easy to scoff at such beliefs and practices, but traditional healers in all cultures are often successful. Leaving aside surgical interventions and the treatment of broken bones, a large part of modern medicine involves helping the patients to heal themselves. If witch doctors can do this through such faith-healing interventions, then they are surely providing a valuable service. Nevertheless, it still surprised me when, at my first place of work, a useful employee could not be dissuaded from resigning his job. This was so that he could comply with a Sangoma's instructions to go up into the hills and carry out various rituals, in order to overcome whatever it was that was troubling him. We never saw that man again.

In African society, getting married could be a very expensive affair for the bridegroom and his family. This is due to the custom of "Lobola", which means "bride price". It refers to the amount that has to be paid by the husband's family to the wife's family, before the wedding can take place. Traditionally this was in cattle, with the final sum being determined by negotiations between the senior members of the two parties. A settlement of 10 cows was typical, but this could be converted into a monetary value, and paid wholly or partly in cash. Various factors could influence the "value" of the bride, including her educational level, and the loss of income that she was contributing to her parents' household.

For a custom like this to have originated in the first place, there would have been obvious benefits for both families. With an economy based largely on agriculture, a person's wealth would have been measured by how many cattle they owned. Handing over a few of these animals to the bride's parents need not have been unduly punitive. The girl's parents would have been compensated for the loss of a valued daughter, whereas the bridegroom would have "bought" a "resource" that would add value to his side of the family. But what about the situation today? Few Africans have their own farms, and the majority live in townships and work in factories. If they have one or more sons of marriageable age, it is doubtful that they would possess sufficient funds to buy cattle for the equivalent of a dowry.

When questioned about this, an older man at the biscuit factory said that sometimes parents try to help the young couple make a good start in their new life, rather than insist on the lobola obligation. Whilst it was not our business to question traditions that were unfamiliar to us, we did think that the time may have arrived when this practice should be revised, to take into account the current economic climate.

In order to try and learn more about how the local marriage customs operate today, Ellen, one of the girls at the factory told me about some of the stages of preparation she would have to go through for her own forthcoming wedding. It all sounded very complicated. Ellen said that the first step is for the boy's parents to visit the girl's parents, to discuss lobola. This would depend partly on the girl's potential earnings, but it appeared that the typical sum agreed had come down somewhat from the days when 10 cows was the norm. The range was now generally 250 to 1,000 rands, although this still represented from two to 10 months' average wage for a black worker. Ellen then continued, "The girl then buys special clothes for the boy's parents: a jacket for his father, and a blanket for his mother." Although a blanket may seem an unusual item of clothing, the African ladies often wore them around their waists.

"What happens after that?" was my next question.

"The girl then buys her future husband some soap and a towel; this shows that he will be a married man." The origin of this rather novel tradition remained unexplained. Ellen continued, "The boy only goes to meet the girl's parents on the second or third meeting between the two families."

"The parents settle the date of the wedding, which is usually held on a Saturday. During the church ceremony, special songs are sung, and the groom puts rings on his bride's fingers. Afterwards there is a celebration lunch, where presents are given to the couple." What then followed was a little surprising to me. "In the evening, when the party is over, the bride and groom each go back to the home of their respective parent's." Why should this be? Again, no explanation was offered. Presumably the reasons for this tradition were now lost in history.

The story continued, "At 12 noon the next day, which would be a Sunday, the husband and his parents go and collect the bride, and they all go back to his house. On the second day, the boy's parents go off for the day and leave the newly-weds alone. The bride then lives with her husband's parents until the young couple can obtain their own house, but this could take one or two years."

It was intriguing to hear this elaborate sequence of stages, each of which must have originated for a purpose. In this modern age, some of the rituals seemed to be iniquitous but, if it led to a stable relationship and a happy marriage, then it would be out of order to criticize. But there was yet another element relating to marriage that only came to my notice sometime later. It was that it was advantageous for the girl to prove her fertility by having a baby, *before* marriage. Presumably the idea of a childless union was unacceptable, perhaps because there would be neither any children to support the parents in their old age, nor any girls who could generate lobola.

There was indeed much in the African culture that was based on tradition, which sometimes made it difficult for outsiders like us to understand the reasons for certain behaviors. A belief in faith healers, and the reluctance to demonstrate individualism in the face of tribal solidarity, are just two that have already been discussed. Traditions often develop as survival mechanisms, but then may appear anachronistic when the environment changes, such as urban living replacing life in the bush. Observing such practices nevertheless added richness to our experience of living in a different culture to that in which we were brought up.

One consequence for the local Africans of urban living, working in industry and, hopefully, preparing to take on leadership roles once democratization eventually came, was the need for a good education. In theory, schools in the townships were supposed to provide a similar level of teaching to that available for white children. In practice, the funding and other resources allocated to the black schools were woefully inadequate. Our local church tried to help by devoting Saturdays to help township pupils prepare for their school-leaving matriculation examinations. Members of the congregation who were teachers gave freely of their time to coach the children. With not being a teacher, my own contribution was instead to provide a free vocational guidance testing service for these youngsters.

This procedure required the participants to complete several questionnaires that could be used to assess aptitudes, interests and personality. In addition, the children were interviewed to see what their present preferences might be with regard to future employment. The forms were processed during the intervening week, so that feedback could be given the following Saturday. What was of particular interest to me was the high number of times that doctors and lawyers were stated as being the favored occupations. The reasons appeared to be that these two professions were seen as being most helpful to the black people in their disadvantaged situation. Any jobs remotely related to security, policing or the armed services were hated. This was a very sad consequence of what these people were going through under the apartheid system.

The pupils hardly ever listed typical occupations in industry or commerce, almost certainly because they had little knowledge of what such jobs entailed. The vocational guidance tests rarely confirmed that these students were suitable candidates for doctors or lawyers. As might be expected, the outcomes mostly suggested jobs in manufacturing, warehousing, retailing, book keeping, and technology. Rather than being disappointed by recommendations such as these, the reaction was usually one of delight at now having some advice on what jobs to seek, once their schooling had been completed.

Susan helped in two of the other initiatives inaugurated by the church. The first was being one of those who taught African maidservants to read and write in English. Unfortunately, many of these women had not been to school, and so had not learned these primary skills. Most white households employed domestic help, and were happy to let them attend a literary class for one afternoon a week. Susan found this work very rewarding, and was very moved when the ladies expressed their thanks by singing in the beautiful way that comes so naturally to these people.

The second activity with which my wife was involved was in helping to make up regular food parcels for the neediest residents of Daveyton, the local township of Benoni. This involved seeking donations of staple foodstuffs that included maize meal, sugar, tea, milk powder, peanut butter, soup powder, and tinned goods, or negotiating discounts for these from suppliers. The parcels were then put together by a team of volunteers. The church owned a van about the size of a minibus, and a volunteer was needed to drive it into Daveytown, and drop the parcels off at several locations. On the occasions when it was Susan's turn to deliver the donations, the driving duty fell to me. Fortunately, my employer was kind enough to allow time off to do it.

Driving into a black township required police permission, as was described in chapter 5, and might have seemed risky for two white people travelling alone. There were, however, no worries on that score for us. We always felt safe because the church van had emblazoned on each side the words: "Beware, saints in transit!"

Although the greatest cultural difference to our own lay with the indigenous African population, it was surprising how many Afrikaans expressions, whether in their English translations or the original language, our family adopted. We compared notes with our three sons only recently. The regular warning, heard on the radio during the height of the government banning orders: "It will not be tolerated" has already been mentioned, as has Braaivleis (burnt meat/ barbeque) and laat lammetjie (late lamb/baby).

We also invariably greet each other with "How's it?" or the Afrikaans version "Hoe gaan dit?" ("How are you?"). A friendly way to address a young boy is "boytjie", which translates as "lad" or "a bit of a lad", and our older sons often refer to each other as "boet" (brother). Then there is the ubiquitous "lekker", the meanings of which can include: "sweet" (including, in the plural, sweets themselves), "nice", "fun", "tasty", and "good" (as in response to "How are you?", and sexy (as in a man commenting about a woman). "Domkop" means "dumb head", and "houtkop" "wooden head", both being handy expressions to use if you want to insult somebody. As was mentioned earlier, it was also useful to be able to recognize some Afrikaans swearwords, just to know when you were being insulted, but you would not want me to list them here, would you?

This is not an exhaustive list by any means, but our continued use of such expressions is an interesting confirmation of how readily, and subconsciously, one can become absorbed into a different culture.

It took us quite a long time to accept that, when telephoning a person to ask when they will be coming to see you, the response, "Just now" was likely to mean they will not come at all. If the reply was "Now, now", then they will come when they feel like it. My memory of an Afrikaans boss who was quite a character includes one of his favorite sayings, "Jah well, no, fine". This brilliant literary jewel was frequently used by him to respond to questions and comments for which he did not have a specific answer. It certainly covered all eventualities, and he could never be accused of being wrong!

The colloquial name for a man was "Oke", sometimes even shortened still further just to "O". A line of comic song reads something like for following:

"In Beaufort West there's an O with a chest
Of six foot in diameter."

So far, nobody has been able to supply me with the rest of this verse.

Want to hear a corny joke? No? Well here it is anyway:

Question: "What do you call an O living in a tree?

Answer: "A Tree-O"

"Lekker, eh?"

Chapter 15

The Food

ANY DESCRIPTION OF LIFE in South Africa would not be complete without a discussion on food. The first meal we ever had in this country—a lunch in Cape Town—turned out to be a good example of the healthy, wholesome eating with which we would become familiar in the years that followed. My wife, Susan, is the best family member to write on this topic, and she enthusiastically accepted my invitation to contribute to this chapter.

Before handing the pen (or rather the keyboard these days) over to her, here are just a few of my own memories. Once we had moved to Benoni, and settled in our first house there, it seemed a good idea to sample the local restaurants. On our first visit to one of them, we ordered our meal and then asked to see the wine list—we had already developed a liking for the excellent, and modestly-priced, local produce. The other diners around us already looked to be enjoying there glasses of plonk.

The waiter responded, "Sorry, we are not licensed to serve alcohol." Before we had the chance to express our disappointment, he continued, "But I can fix you up."

"We don't understand, do you have a wine list, or not?" was my rather naïve reply.

"No, we are not licensed, but I can fix you up", he repeated.

The penny still had not dropped, and the next question was, "What sort of wine can you fix us up with?"

The Food

After some further negotiation, we asked for a bottle of dry white, which duly arrived and was much enjoyed. It was only some time later that it eventually dawned on us that there were some under-the-counter dealings going on at this eatery. It appeared that at least some of the other customers had brought their own liqueur with them. Now that we were conversant with the system at that restaurant, and to avoid any more confusion, the next time we went there, we took our own bottle of wine with us. Lo and behold! We were politely informed that they now had a liqueur license, and that we could not drink our own booze! Ah well, it was just part of our learning curve, but the expression: "I can fix you up" remains in our vocabulary to this day.

Everyone has their favorite food, although most of us would not order exactly the same range of dishes every time we went out to a restaurant. An exception was an Afrikaans work friend of mine with whom we dined on a number of occasions, along with his wife. His choice from the menu never varied, and he made it very clear that a more perfect combination of items could not possibly be created. He started off with a prawn cocktail, followed it with steak and chips, and ended with ice cream with hot chocolate sauce. If the establishment could not supply all these, then it was removed from his list of places to revisit. All very nice, but most of us would want a change now and again!

Another food-related memory is not so much related to the joys of eating, but rather the consequences. Upset stomachs were not rare in South Africa, and there was one variety known as "apricot fever" to which several of us succumbed at least once during our stay. It may have been unfair to blame this tasty fruit, but the sickness coincided with the time when apricots were ready for harvesting. One type of large flying insect was also aware of this, and tended to make a bee-line (sorry for the pun) for the ripe fruits. What they may have been standing in before visiting the apricots is perhaps best left unknown. Many gardens had one or more of these trees, and it was very tempting to just pluck one of the orange delicacies and eat it, without washing it first. It is not surprising, therefore, that nausea and its associated symptoms could follow a day or so later.

The family doctors were familiar with this, and had a very effective routine treatment. You were led into a spare room at the surgery, and put on an intravenous drip that contained two additives: Valoid to control the nausea, and Buscopan to deal with the stomach spasms. An hour later, you walked from the surgery, feeling many times better. The next time a person who had been through this routine picked an apricot from a tree, he or she made sure that they washed it first!

Just one more memory to share with you before handing over to Susan—and not an appetizing one for me—concerns what some of the hard-up Africans ate. It just emphasizes how picky we are when we have a modest income, compared with how those with limited means ensure that nothing goes to waste. This was often reflected in the rather dubious (to a Brit's eyes, anyway) cuts of meat that were eaten along with the ubiquitous maize meal.

When doing my rounds of the plastics molding machines at my last place of work, one operator appeared to be eating something in the gaps between having to take completed items from his machine. Closer inspection revealed that he had a cooked sheep's head, and was using a sharp knife to shave bits of flesh off the skull and pop them into his mouth when the opportunity arose. Susan has just reminded me that these cranial delicacies were usually referred to by their Afrikaans name: "Skappie". Useful to keep this in mind if you visit the country, and wish to try (or avoid) this nutritious food for yourself.

Well, that is my contribution to this chapter on food, so now over to Susan for a proper description of the gastronomic delights of South Africa.

> There is a shelf in the tiny, galley-style kitchen of where we live now in the UK. In one corner, there are a couple of my favorite recipe books. The one I use the most (it's obvious because of the many greasy finger marks that cover it) is called "Favorite Recipes". It was published by the "Prevention of Cruelty to Animals" society of Swaziland,

The Food

and comprises contributions from ordinary housewives who had been asked to send in their favorite recipes. They make up a beautiful, yummy mixture, encompassing the very best of South African food. A foodie's delight!

So many different people brought their best food traditions with them when they arrived in South Africa: the Portuguese, Greek, Indian, Chinese, Cape Malay, Dutch, and British. Added to these are the indigenous populations of different African tribes: Zulu, Sotho, and Xhosa, to name the main ones. This has resulted in some of the best food you will find anywhere in the world. Certainly, when we left South Africa in 1995, there wasn't anything like the reliance there on convenience and ready-meals that there is in the UK. On our first trip to the supermarket after our return to Blighty, we couldn't believe the number of ready-meals on display at eye-watering prices. None of that for the average South African, just fresh food, cooked either inside or outdoors, depending on the season.

Certainly the family's favorite food in South Africa was the braaivleis. Not very appetizing, you might think, but absolutely delicious. We all still enjoy this as often as our British summer will allow. It has become traditional for the Lowis tribe to gather en masse, here in Northampton in August, for what has become known as the family braai. Our numbers continue to increase as the sons find wives and girlfriends, and the grandchildren have started to come along. Long may it continue!

The next favorite food after the braai just has to be the Melktert, which is made to another Afrikaans recipe. It is similar to the good old English Custard Tart, but has a richer egg custard that is stirred in the pan first, and then poured into the tart when cooked. The finishing touch is a sprinkling of cinnamon on top, not nutmeg. The closest way to describe this is that it is the same filling as you get in crème patisserie in a short crust pastry case.

The Portuguese brought their Peri-Peri spice with them. This resulted in a chain of chicken restaurants starting up while we were in South Africa in the eighties. Readers will be familiar with the name "Nandos" eateries, which are rife all over the UK now. Very tasty chicken it is too! However, no doubt the family will agree that the best thing to come out of Portugal in our time in South Africa was the Portuguese bread roll. There is nothing like it here in the UK, nor in Portugal as far as I can see, in the short time we have spent there on holiday. These had to be bought from the café around the corner on the day you were going to eat them. An essential part of any good braai.

Greengrocers were mostly run by the Portuguese community, and the amount of fresh produce on display was a delight to behold. Oh and so cheap too! Whole boxes of mangos could be bought for the equivalent of about two British pounds. Greek salad was another indispensable part of any barbie or cold buffet. Cape Malay food was probably the most interesting, and certainly different, fare available. It comprised lots of curries and spices, but was quite different from the Indian curries with which the British would be more familiar. There was quite a lot of fruit in these recipes, and chutney too, so they turned out to be a lot sweeter than an Indian curry. One of the most common of such dishes was something called "Bobotie." This comprised a mince curry, thickened with breadcrumbs' and an egg custard poured over the top. It was then baked in the oven. Whilst this might sound a strange combination, it was very tasty and not too hot.

The main place for a really good Indian curry was Durban. Many people came over from India in the late nineteenth century, to work in the cotton fields and sugar cane plantations. They brought their cuisine with them. We have many happy memories of holidays at the Salt Rock Hotel, just north of Durban, where a curry would be a choice on the menu most evenings. The best thing was the Sambals that came with it. These were a bit like the poppadums that are served in UK Indian restaurants at the start of a meal. They usually came with pickles and other tasty morsels.

Traditional African cooking relied heavily on maize meal to bulk everything out. This was locally known as "pap". Chuck steak was the favorite meat whenever it could be afforded. It was always served on the bone and eaten with the fingers. The meat was cooked in a tomato and onion gravy, so the pap was useful for mopping up the juices.

The Food

"Boerewors"—literally "Afrikaans sausage"—also went well with the pap and gravy. These were made out of beef, rather than pork, and each variety had its own special seasoning. "Bunny Chow" was something that husband Mike had discovered in his first job at the bread bakery (see chapter 4). This comprised a loaf with the middle scooped out, and the space filled with anything savory that was available. Great for eating on the run!

Over the years it was my good fortune to have several African ladies to help me in the house. Many of them were interested in cooking and eager to know what English people ate. My memory is of teaching a few of them to make mince pies at Christmas, and they were very proud to have something they could make for the family that was typically English. The teaching was mutually beneficial, and many culinary tips were picked up from these ladies to add to my personal recipe book. Talking of Christmas, this happened at the hottest time of the year, but we were amazed to find that nearly all South Africans who could lay any claim to British ancestry, insisted on cooking the whole roast turkey dinner thing. We could never understand this and the most I ever did was to cook the blessed meal on Christmas Eve evening, when it was a bit cooler. Then we had the whole thing cold again on Christmas Day. Phew!

The Chinese brought their own type of oriental cuisine with them and, as in Britain, going out for a Chinese was considered a real treat. Other than that, they were one of the few groups of people who didn't seem to integrate very well, and they tended to keep themselves to themselves. Some other eating-out experiences that were very special and, surprisingly, not too expensive, revolved around the seafood, especially when we were on holiday at the coast. Mike and I still drool over the wonderful lobster thermidor we enjoyed at the Chaka's Rock Hotel on the Zululand coast, very close to our Salt Rock holiday haunt. The prawns too were amazing, very large and juicy. Never found anything like them here. Ah, Happy Days!

Chapter 16

Diversion
The day the Pope saved my life

No doubt we have all had a day that we shall never forget, maybe one that was life-changing. The most memorable day for me occurred on 30th September, 1979, and it involved the pope of that time—albeit indirectly. Whilst what follows is not a description of something that actually happened *in* South Africa itself, it did occur during the 20 years we lived there. It therefore seems justified to include it in this book, especially as it is arguably one of the most memorable events of my life to date.

Pope John Paul ll was the first non-Italian in more than 400 years to attain this office. His real name was Karol Józef Wojyla; he was born in Poland in 1920, and ordained in 1964. Three years later, Pope Paul VI made Wojyla a cardinal and, in 1978, he succeeded his predecessor John Paul l and became the 264th pope. During his tenure he was a popular and charismatic leader of the Catholic Church, and an active campaigner for human rights. He also had strong views on a number of issues, including opposition to both capital punishment and contraception. Despite his popularity, in 1981 John Paul was the victim of an assassination attempt, whilst in St. Peter's Square in Vatican City. Although being shot four times, he made a successful recovery.

The motivation for this is not known, but some believe it may have been because of his support of solidarity in his home country of Poland, at a time of attempted communist domination. Amazingly, in the following year, there was a second assassination attempt, this time in Fatima, Portugal, carried out by a fanatical priest. On this occasion the pope received several knife wounds. John Paul was believed to have suffered from Parkinson's disease in his later years, and he in died in Italy in 2005, aged 84.

The pope travelled widely to spread his message of faith and peace. It was fortunate for me that, on 30th September, 1979, it included his visit to Ireland, the first ever made by a pope to that country. This was during the time of my employment with the pharmaceuticals manufacturing company, situated near Soweto. As was mentioned in chapter 13, it was one of the large firms with international connections that encouraged overseas visits, to help keep up to date with the latest technology.

The American auditors had invited me to join them in their inspection of their manufacturing facility in Castlebar, which is situated in County Mayo, to the north-west of Ireland, and my employer had agreed to let me go. The plan was to first fly to London, meet up with the team leader, and spend the night there in a hotel. This went according to plan and, the following morning, we flew to Shannon airport. Once there, the intention was that we would be joined by the other two auditors, who would have flown in from the USA.

This was the very day of the pope's historic visit. He had just arrived in Dublin, and television screens had been placed all around the airport lounge to relay every moment of the event to passengers who had the opportunity to linger for a while. The two of us had time to watch some of this coverage, whilst awaiting the arrival of our colleagues, and it was clear that the event had generated widespread enthusiasm and euphoria. All the streets were lined with bunting, which included the distinctive yellow papal flags. There was an opportunity later for me to buy one of these as a souvenir, and it is still in my possession to remind me of this significant day in my life. The plan was that, once the others had arrived, the four of us would complete the journey to the factory in a small aircraft that had been chartered for this purpose.

Things then started to go wrong. The rest of the team were not on the scheduled flight that arrived from the USA. When this became clear, the team leader said that our chartered aircraft could not be delayed. The two of us would have to complete the journey alone. Assuming that the other auditors arrived on a later flight, they would then have to join us by whatever means they could.

We boarded the little plane, and the pilot took off. By this time, Pope John Paul was either on his way to, or had arrived at, the small town of Knock, to conduct one of the main masses of his visit. This urban area is conveniently situated close to the centre of Southern Ireland, and it was later estimated that 450,000 people attended the event, which represented over 13 percent of the entire population of that country. As might be expected, the level of security was very high: not only were there road blocks all around Knock, but no aircraft were permitted to fly over the town whilst the pope was present.

Our original flight plan was to fly north, passing over Knock, and land on a short grass landing strip next to the Castlebar factory. Shortly after take-off, the pilot announced, "Because of the flight restrictions, we would have to take a westward loop over the sea, and then turn back toward the land for our approach to the factory runway. The flight would therefore take about 20 minutes longer than the direct route." Although we were not particularly happy with this delay, we appreciated the reason and just resigned ourselves to a longer journey.

Despite the drizzle on the windows, and the rather ominous view of the boiling sea beneath us, we had an uneventful journey until we were on the approach to the landing strip. Our pilot then made another announcement. He said, "The weather has suddenly deteriorated, a mist was closing in, and visibility was poor." What followed was news that we certainly did not want to hear: "Because the landing strip is unmanned, there is no radar or other guidance system. In the interests of safety, there is no alternative but to turn around and return to Shannon airport." It was little consolation when he commented that, had we been able to fly the direct route, there would have been just enough time for him to land, let us alight, and then take off before the weather closed in.

Diversion

You can imagine how we felt about this, but obviously we had to accept the situation. After a tedious return journey, we eventually approached Shannon and touched down. A few seconds later, as the pilot started to apply the brakes, the plane started to shake violently. He released the brakes and the aircraft steadied, but the shaking began again whenever he tried to slow down. The pilot then radioed the control tower, saying that he would have to freewheel until the plane came to a natural halt. Fortunately, the Shannon runway is one of the longest in the British Isles, and the air traffic controller ensured that no other plane tried to land behind us. After what seemed to be an age, but in reality was probably less than a minute, we came to a stop, got out and had a look at the plane.

The pilot found that the supporting structure for the front wheel mounting had broken, so that every time the brakes were applied the plane tipped forward and became unstable. He said it was just lucky that the runway was long enough to let him freewheel to a stop. If he had been able to attempt a landing at the very short factory airstrip, the plane would have either somersaulted when the brakes were applied, or crashed into buildings at the end of the grass strip. There would not have been the opportunity to either free wheel to a halt, or try and take off again. Either way, we would have been very lucky to escape with our lives.

The reality of this started to sink in. If we had not had the delay flying over the sea to avoid Knock where the pope was, we would have attempted a landing on the strip next to the factory—with disastrous consequences. Were we just lucky? Was this only a coincidence? Or was it meant to be that John Paul was there for us just when we needed him?

There is a postscript to this story, as what followed later was as meaningful for me as was the narrowly-avoided accident, but in a completely different way. By the time we returned to Shannon, the other two auditors had arrived from the USA on a later plane. The leader said we would now have to take a taxi for the quite long drive up to the hotel in County Mayo.

It was now late in the afternoon. My feelings at that time comprised a rather confused mixture of, on the one hand, the nervy after-effects of our morning's adventure and, on the other, being fed up that we would be cramped up in what could be a long taxi journey. It was still drizzling and also getting dark; many roads remained closed because of the pope's presence. It was going to be a miserable journey. Could it get any worse, I wondered?

We came up against the first road block as we approached the outskirts of Knock, which was still in a state of high security. Were we about to be told to turn around and only try again several hours later? The taxi driver impressed us with his skill in being able to convince the police that we were not a security risk, and that we just wanted to proceed to our ultimate destination as quickly as possible. Bravo for him!

During the taxi journey, my self-question on whether the situation could get any worse was answered by the team leader—yes, it could! He had been to our Castlebar hotel before, so he knew how it operated. "We would arrive too late for dinner", he said, adding with small comfort. "But I hope that the proprietor will be able to rustle up a sandwich or something before we go to bed." This certainly did nothing to raise the spirits. At long last, in the dark, we turned into the grounds of the hotel. Looming up ahead of us was the outline of a building that could have been used for the film "*Psycho.*" I don't think it would have been possible to be filled with more doom and gloom about what was surely in store for us.

But then, as we drew up to the building, a door opened revealing a bright, almost ethereal light. A man came out to the car and gave us a warm welcome, saying that he realized we would be late and that he had delayed dinner until our arrival. We were ushered inside, and into the cheerful dining room with a long table already filling up with food and bottles of wine. The transformation from being at the lowest ebb to a feeling of joy and happiness was instant, and one of the most remarkable transformations of my life—a genuine epiphany! It was a wonderful meal that included local salmon, and there was good company and laughter. A truly remarkable day, but one that would not have ended happily without Pope John Paul ll. Indeed, it was a day I shall never forget.

Chapter 17

The First Democratic Elections

As FATE WOULD HAVE it, we were living in South Africa during some of the darkest days of the apartheid era, as well as the move toward democratization that culminated in the first fully inclusive elections. Thus we were able to witness first-hand the events that many outside the country could only hear about via the various media presentations which, unfortunately, were not always delivered free of bias. In total, the various black racial groups comprised about 80 percent of the population. On the principle of majority rule, it is clear that they had the right to form the government. Does historical evidence confirm the legitimacy of this claim?

It may be helpful to have a brief look at how the socio-political situation in South Africa unfolded over time. A potted history of human occupation in this country was included in chapter 4. Yes, the San ("Bushmen") people were there first, and other BaNtu (black) tribes migrated southwards sometime later. Whilst this clarifies who were the first inhabitants of the country, some may say that there would have been no progress without the input of people from other nations. Although some European sailors may have briefly called at the Cape earlier, the first white settlers, from Holland, only arrived in 1652. People from other nations, including Britain, followed.

For nearly the next 100 years, everybody seemed to be fighting everybody else. The British fought the Zulus, and there were two Anglo-Boer wars. The Afrikaners started their Great Trek northwards in 1835, to try and escape from British domination. The discovery of diamonds in Kimberly (1866), and gold in the Witwatersrand (1884), however, only served to strengthen the resolve of the British, who had settled in these areas in order to control the lucrative mining industries.

In the year 1910, after much political wrangling, the Union of South Africa was formed with the unification of the Cape, Natal, Transvaal, and Orange River colonies previously under British control. Although the country was officially a British dominion, with an appointed governor-general, in practice it was self-governing. The parliament was Afrikaans dominated, and the prime minister was an ex Boer general, Louis Botha.

This situation remained until 1961, when South Africa declared itself a republic, left the Commonwealth, and appointed a state president. The role was largely ceremonial at that time, and executive powers remained with the prime minister. Just to add to the confusion, in 1984 (at the time we were in the country) the office of prime minister was abolished, and the incumbent at that time—P. W. Botha—was appointed president with executive powers.

Although the first democratic elections were held in 1994, dramatic changes like this do not occur overnight. It was not clear, at least to people like us, what was going on behind the scenes for much of the run-up to the actual election. The Soweto Riots, which occurred in 1976, triggered such a strong reaction both within the country and beyond, that some relaxation of the apartheid stranglehold was inevitable. Nelson Mandela was imprisoned on Robben Island in 1964, after being found guilty, along with others, of plotting to overthrow the government. In 1982, whilst P. W. Botha was still prime minister, Mandela was transferred to a less-harsh mainland prison. There was some contact between him and government representatives over the next year or two, and this culminated in a meeting with Botha in 1989.

We can only guess what was discussed, but it must have included the topic of a future democratic South Africa. Shortly after

The First Democratic Elections

this, F. W. de Klerk succeeded Botha as president, and he had the first of what must have been several discussions with Mandela. Only a month or two later, there was a dramatic announcement in a news bulletin: Nelson Mandela was to be released on 11th February, 1990.

On the day of this announcement, Susan and I went for an evening meal at our favorite restaurant in Benoni. When the black waiter was asked if he had heard the news that Mandela was to be released from prison, rather than look delighted, he exhaled a sigh of resignation and said, "This will just be another trick of the government to keep us quiet, and it will not be really true."

"No", we assured him. "This is for real, he will be released on 11th February." The poor waiter still seemed unconvinced, but no doubt went off to share the news with his colleagues in the kitchen.

We enjoyed our (rather small) lobster thermidor on special offer, price 10 rands, which was much less than the equivalent in British pounds. Our pleasure was considerably enhanced by the knowledge that, not only was the journey toward democratization definitely under way for the whole nation, but that we were the first to break the good news to our skeptical waiter. If he did not fully believe us at this moment, he would definitely do so the next morning when the story would be in all the newspapers.

Events soon gained momentum. On 2nd February, nine days before Mandela was due to be released, President de Klerk lifted restrictions on a wide range of opposition groups. As the day drew closer, the excitement among most of the population grew ever stronger. Of course, there would be those, especially extreme right-wing Afrikaners, who opposed the freeing of a man they still regarded as a potential terrorist, and who would wreak vengeance on his oppressors, given the chance. For most of us, it would be an event that should ultimately lead to peace and prosperity for all.

One thing that added to the interest was that, for the entire duration of Mandela's imprisonment, it was strictly illegal to print any image of his current appearance. This rule was never rescinded, and all that was available were photographs taken at the time of his trial 27 years earlier. We were all keen to see what he looked like now and, if he gave a speech, what he sounded like. Naturally, there was full television coverage, and many countries outside South Africa would be seeing the event live. The tension mounted as the hour of his release drew nearer.

Mandela's wife, Winnie, went into the prison to spend a short time with her husband. We then heard that the pair had left the building and were walking toward the prison gates, into the area where crowds were waiting and the cameras were installed. At last, there he was, a man of slim build, grey hair, and with a few wrinkles, as one would expect of someone aged 71. He walked with dignity, but we cannot recall seeing the ready smile for which he was well known later. The television camera positions were obviously not ideal; they must have been placed some distance away from the action, relying on zoom lenses for the closer images.

Mandela reached a raised platform, and addressed the crowds. It was only due to a courageous cameraman who, we later learned, was perilously perched on top of a ladder, that viewers had any pictures of this part of the proceedings. For me, the speech was rather disappointing, and my recollection is mostly of him commending those who were jailed along with himself, or who were left-wing activists. Maybe we missed something, but some thanks for those who had helped secure his release, along with a few words of commitment to work for peace and prosperity for all, would have been nice to hear. Still, he had been behind bars for all those years, so perhaps he could be forgiven for such omissions.

Whilst violence in the country did not immediately cease, negotiations toward agreement of a new constitution progressed, with 19 political parties taking part. It was agreed that the first democratic election would be held in April 1994, extending over three days to ensure that all those in the more remote regions of the country would be able to vote. It was fascinating to witness two distinct types of emotion in the run-up to the ballot. The non-white population was understandably excited that they would at long last have a say in their own government, whilst the moderate whites philosophically accepted that such a democratic change was inevitable, and even long overdue. By contrast, the reaction of the more right-wing individuals sometimes boarded on the ludicrous.

There was a belief among these extremists that, on waking up the day after the elections were over, the country would have somehow changed and that all public services and resources would immediately cease. This led to a hording of elements considered to be indispensible to life, including electric generators, as much food, water and other essentials as could be accommodated and, inevitably, weapons. Susan heard a radio phone-in program where listeners were suggesting what essentials to stock-pile. These ranged from baked beans on the one hand, to wine and whisky on the other. It became a joke within our family that the thing to do in times of emergency was, like these prophets of doom, to stock up with toilet rolls and tins of tuna fish!

The election was duly held from the 26th to 28th of April, 1994. These three days were declared national holidays, to ensure that everyone would be free to travel to a polling station which, in some rural areas, could be a lengthy journey. Susan had volunteered to be a helper at one of the voting centers, and she accepted my invitation to write about this experience in her own words. Here is her report:

> It was 6am on Wednesday the 27th April 1994 at a voting office just outside Benoni where we lived.
>
> April in South Africa is as beautiful as it is in the UK. Everything is still so green after the summer rains. The rain had stopped now over the Highveld and it probably wouldn't rain again until September. The air was already dry and crisp, but very cold so early in the morning. However, by 11 am it would be very pleasantly warm, lower twenties centigrade, just right. It's such a relief after the intense heat in the height of summer. February can be incredibly hot and humid, March a bit better but April is just perfect.
>
> So how was it that a middle-aged English woman like me came to be working as a voting official at the first fully democratic election that South Africa had ever had? It had been a very long and difficult road before this

day dawned. There were times when it didn't seem as if it could ever happen. It was four years after the release of Nelson Mandela. Four very difficult years, with talks about talks about talks that rarely reached any conclusions. Once a date had finally been set, this seemed to be a signal for all the different war-mongering parties to see who could get the upper hand. The Inkatha Freedom party, led by Zulu Chief Buthelezi, was the main culprit. The violence and bloodshed that took place in the weeks running up to the elections was extremely disturbing. Many lives were lost, and we thought there could be no way that voting would take place in any sort of calm and peaceful atmosphere.

The African National Congress party (ANC), which had the greatest following among the black population, and Inkatha, seemed to have had irreconcilable differences. This resulted in Buthelezi initially refusing to take part in the elections, but he changed his mind just a few weeks before they were scheduled. The voting papers had already been printed by then, with each of the numerous political parties being represented by an image—usually a picture of the leader—for the benefit of those who could not read the names. After Buthelezi's late decision to participate, 30 million stickers of his mugshot had to be printed and, on the day of the elections, stuck on to the bottom of each of the very long voting slips! See Figure 1 for a photograph of the ballet paper.

So there we had two very proud groups of people, both determined to come out on top in these forthcoming elections. Apart from that, there were many smaller groups who each thought they deserved a share in the pot. In all, I remember there were 19 parties to choose from on the extremely long voting slip.

Once a date had been set, I felt I had to have a part in this. We had lived nearly 20 years in South Africa by this time. We had never become South African Citizens but had remained as Permanent Residents only. Of course our immigrant two elder sons had been forcibly made South African citizens, when the Nationalist government of the day decided that they needed to be conscripted into their army. Peter had returned to England to avoid this.

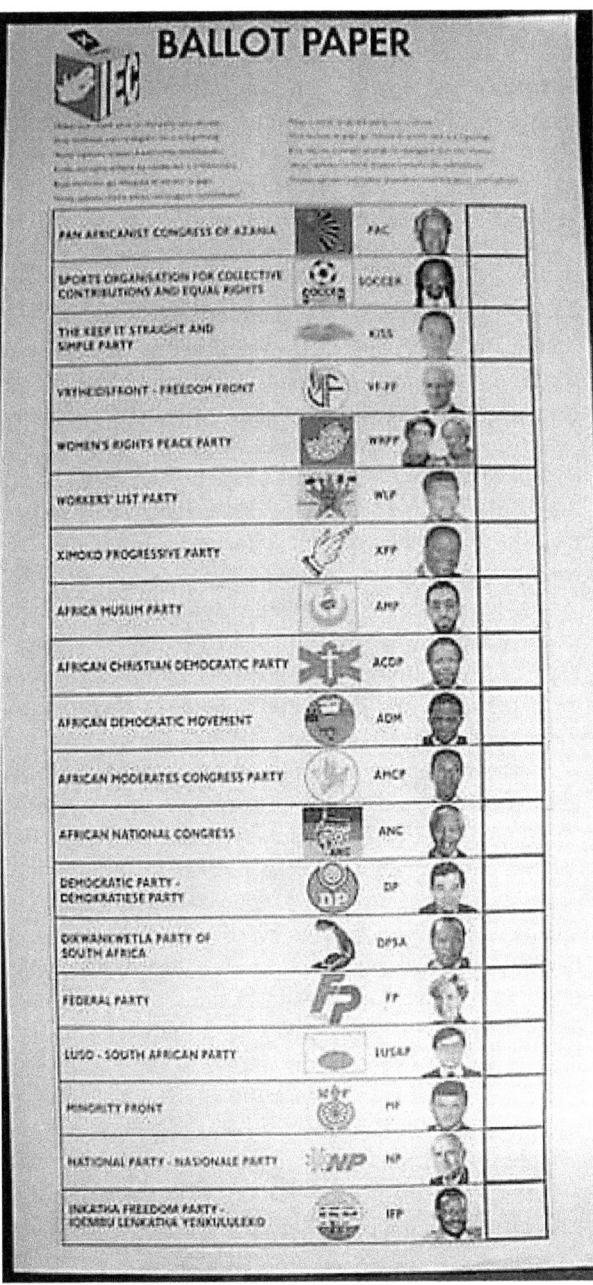

Figure 1. The ballot paper for the first democratic elections

David would have done the same, but the powers-that-be lost his papers so he didn't bother to remind them of his existence. I could never understand just what it was this army was supposed to be defending. I asked many white, South African mums of sons this question and they said their borders had to be protected.

So there I was on the 27th April. The day had finally come and guess what? There was no violence, and everything was peaceful on that cold and rather misty dawn on the Highveld. What there was outside of the polling station was a line of people that stretched as far as the eye could see. I couldn't see the end of the queue, but they had obviously been there from very, very early in the morning, long before I was up and about. The people were quiet, they were dignified, they were peaceful, they smiled, and they looked relieved and happy! Many were wrapped in blankets to keep the cold out. Some had hats and scarves, prized possessions among the African people.

At last the doors were opened and the queue started to move forward. Would there be a rush now? A riot perhaps? But no, the same patience the same resignation, the same quiet dignity prevailed. Some of them kissed the paper before placing it into the Ballot Box. There was very little conversation, though, almost a reverence, a bit like being in Church and taking communion.

One old lady, I do remember, looked at me and said, "Now I have my dignity back." I say 'old lady'; she was probably in her seventies! I remember thinking, how terrible it must have been to get to such a great age and never to have had the vote. I couldn't stop myself thinking that in some way I was to blame for allowing it to happen. For we were all guilty of sitting back and saying, "What can I do?" It was so easy to relax in the sun and enjoy all that such a beautiful country had to offer, without really thinking about the sort of life our African neighbors had lived.

I had had many conversations over the years with African ladies about the politics there and what might happen in the future. Many of them didn't seem all that interested. Like women the world over, their first thought was for their family, and where the next shirt or

The First Democratic Elections

pair of shoes was coming from for their children to wear to school. Only one lady, who was probably in her fifties, had any opinion.

Her name was Diana, and I think she was fortunate in that her education was somewhat better than that of many others. Lots of the women couldn't read or write. Education was for the boys, not the girls. Girls were fully occupied in caring for home and family, and reading and writing wasn't something considered in the least necessary. I asked Diana, how she would feel if Nelson Mandela ever became the President. She sighed, and said, "Oh, Mrs. Sue, they're all politicians and politicians are all the same, just talk!" We laughed. I wonder how she feels now, if she is still alive.

So the 27th of April finally ended as it had started, very peacefully and quietly, and voting continued for another two days without any trouble. In total, nearly twenty million people voted. Then the counting finally started, which couldn't be hurried either; it seemed to take an eternity before the result was declared. As expected, the ANC was proclaimed the winner with nearly two thirds of the vote. Nelson Mandela was finally sworn in as President and so his "Long Walk to Freedom" had ended. Because the National Party had achieved 20 percent of the votes, F. W. de Klerk was appointed one of two deputy presidents. To the surprise of many of the fanatics, the world did continue to exist when we woke up the next morning!

Chapter 18

Life after the Election

IT IS IMPORTANT TO point out that, in the first elections of this kind in South Africa, there were no constituencies or local parliamentary candidates. Instead, people just voted for the political party of their choice. Under the proportional representation system, each leader then appointed a number of MPs based on the percentage of the total votes cast for their party. Thus, for example, the ANC achieved 62.6 percent of the votes, and were then able to appoint a majority 252 representatives to the 400-seat National Assembly. The National Party headed by de Klerk appointed 82 members, and Inkatha 43. In total, 19 parties contested the elections, but only seven of them obtained sufficient votes to be able to nominate MPs.

The smallest representation was from the African Christian Democratic Party (ACDP), whose half of one percent of the votes entitled them to two members. A work associate of mine, who was a Born Again Christian, was particularly pleased that this minority party was represented, because it was the only one that included in its manifesto the banning of pornography. Anything considered even vaguely pornographic had been strictly outlawed under the previous regime. A colleague who visited my company from Australia was very fortunate not to have been severely fined for bringing a copy of *Playboy* magazine with him. The general belief was that the new government would be much more tolerant of such things, so the ACDP was the only hope for those wanting to preserve the old restrictions.

When the list of new MPs was announced, it was perhaps to be expected that a large number of them comprised freedom fighters and political activists. This was regardless of whether or not they had any experience or relevant training to qualify them for government, or had even achieved a good level of education. After any General Election, there will be new members on a steep learning curve, before they can perform in their new roles. There will, however, usually still be a large majority of older hands who can maintain stability, as well as guide the newcomers.

But in the new South African parliament, the only experienced politicians were those of the opposition National Party who had served in the previous government. Would the 80 percent of new members wish to learn from their white predecessors, or would they just follow their own inclinations? We were concerned about this, but hoped that common sense would prevail, along with a dedication to put the interests of the country first.

Whilst the previous prophets of doom worried about how they were going to dispose of their stockpiles of toilet rolls and tins of tuna fish, my family, the rest of the country, and many other countries of the world, waited with optimism to see what the new government would do to reverse the inequality and oppression that had prevailed for so many years. Unfortunately, perusing the names of those in the new government that we recognized did little to inspire confidence, but we knew it would be hasty to prejudge until we had seen just what changes would be made.

One of the first things to be announced after the election was that there would be a massive celebration party in Cape Town for all the new MPs, and others who were deemed to be worthy of a reward for their loyalty and support during the dark days. This would be a lavish affair, with no expense spared. Okay, we thought, letting off some steam and having a good time in these circumstances was only to be expected. Our vicarious joy was somewhat dampened when we heard that a decree had been issued, stating that a not insignificant amount of money would be deducted from the salaries of all those earning above a certain minimum. Now this cut-off point appeared to have been carefully calculated to ensure that most white people in employment, but very few blacks, would contribute to the bash. Perhaps this is just how democracy operates, but it did hurt my pocket!

So far we had the concern about the number of inexperienced MPs in the new parliament, and a depleted pay packet to contend with; what was next in store for us? The answer came soon enough—changes to place names. In order to deal with this matter, The South African Geographical Names Council had been established. The previous minority government had followed the practice of naming many buildings, streets, airports and towns after individuals, most of whom were key figures in Afrikaner history. It was understandable that the new majority regime would want to change most of these.

Airport names were the first to be altered, to reflect those of the major cities they served. For example H. F. Verwoerd Airport became Port Elizabeth International Airport, and Ben Schoeman Airport was changed to East London Airport. In the case of Jan Smuts Airport, however, although this was initially renamed Johannesburg International Airport, several years later it was changed again, this time to O. R. Tambo International Airport. Oliver Tambo was a former president of the ANC. This is not the only example now, as the airport at Durban is one of the others to change. It is now: King Shaka International Airport, after the legendary Zulu monarch. Thus, although the Names Council had resolved not to name airports after former politicians and leaders, the temptation to honor their own heroes had obviously been too strong to resist.

Other changes followed. The large province of Transvaal was divided into four regions, with that of the main commercial centre embracing both Johannesburg and, inter alia, our own town of Benoni, being named Gauteng. This means "at the gold" in one of the African languages. Several towns had their names changed. In the north of the country, Potgietersrust became Mokopane, Pietersburg changed to Polokwane, and Louis Trichard to Makhoda. To the east,

Life after the Election

Nelspruit, the last main town before the Kruger Park, became Mbombela, and Piet Retief, near Swaziland, was changed to Emkhondo. Attempts to rename Pretoria have so far been strongly resisted.

Many smaller settlements were also given African names, and sometimes these had to be subsequently revised to correct misspellings. Finally, a large number of streets, especially those in Johannesburg and Pretoria that were previously named after prominent Afrikaners, were changed so as to honor African personalities. Whilst many were not too happy with the loss of familiar and well-loved place names, once again most of us tolerated this as something that the majority government needed to do to show that they were in charge, and were making changes. If this was the worst of what the new regime would bring, then no doubt we could all live with it.

We only remained in South Africa for about 16 months after the elections. This narrative is primarily intended to relate our own personal experiences in that country, and is not a comprehensive and authoritative text book on its recent history. From our perspective, during the first year or so following the elections, we were very relieved that peace had prevailed, and that there was no open warfare between right and left extremists. Credit must go to President Nelson Mandela for carefully steering a non-aggressive middle course that did not rock the boat too much.

What we did observe was a growing confidence among the black Africans to flex their political muscles and stage protests where they deemed it necessary. My own experiences in the workplace, as related in chapter 12, certainly reflected this. In addition to the brazen hostage taking, much of my remaining work role in South Africa was taken up talking to trade union officials and labor law solicitors, and fighting test cases brought by the workforce. As the day of our return to the UK drew nearer, we started to worry that the prosperity promised for all would take longer than the electorate had anticipated. Would the country remain peaceful and stable, we wondered, or would impatience lead to an escalation of violence and bloodshed?

It was difficult to contain a sigh of relief when, on the last day of July, 1995, our plane took off from Johannesburg Airport to return us to the country we once again would call home. Perhaps "our" is too inclusive a word, as there were just three of us on this journey. For one of us—Charles—who was born in South Africa, it would be to start life in a new country. As Susan mentioned in the previous chapter, Peter had already returned to England, mainly to avoid conscription into the armed forces. David was well established in a job, and lived in his own rented property. He chose to remain in Benoni, and to also keep the dog we had at that time. After a further two years, he also decided it was time for him to leave, and he then joined the rest of us in the UK. The dog happily lived out the rest of its life with a good friend of David's.

The final few weeks had not been easy for me at work, and there was the constant fear of unwelcome visitors during the night. As mentioned several times already, our original intention had been to stay in South Africa for just a few years. But we had soon become absorbed with work, the social scene and, in my case, the undertaking of 13 years of part-time higher education study. Twenty years passed before we realized it. Despite the good times, and the friends we had to leave behind, we were glad to be on our way back to the UK, to be reunited with the family and friends we had neglected for so long.

We have now been back in the UK for longer than the time we spent overseas. Nelson Mandela stood down as president in 1999, and one of the deputy presidents, Thabo Mbeki, took over this role. The other deputy president, F. W. de Klerk, resigned his post after only two years in office. Thus, there was no longer a representative of the National Party at this senior level, although it still had MPs in the National Assembly. After just one year of Kgalema Motlanthe being in the post, Jacob Zuma became president in 2009 and was still there at the time or writing, eight years later.

Looking back now, were we right to have concerns that peace and stability in South Africa may have been starting to deteriorate during the final year of our stay? This can only be informed by reference to messages from friends who still live there, along with news items that appear in the media from time to time. Some of these reports might be biased and reflect only a narrow view, but perhaps the selection of comments that follow may help readers form their own opinions.

A few years after our return to the UK, a letter containing a cutting from the *Pretoria News* dropped through our letterbox. The headline read: "Gunmen shoot city lecturer in yet another attack". The story relates to a professor from the University of South Africa who had been shot in the back by gunmen, whilst he was in his garden. The victim was lucky to have been found shortly afterwards by his adult son, who quickly drove him to hospital in time to have his life saved. The report says that the gunmen then jumped over a wall, and held up children who were having a party in the next garden. Wallets and mobile phones were stolen, and the villains fled. A police spokesperson is quoted as saying that this is the fourth such incident in this location in three weeks. Two of the other victims had died. The perpetrators had not been caught.

This story was especially significant to me, as the professor had been my supervisor during the last three years of my studies. What started as an academic association developed into a warm friendship, which included dinner parties, together with our wives. The good news is that the report was sent to me by the man himself, and we still keep in touch by email. Despite his serious injuries, he—an Afrikaner—says that he holds no bitterness toward his callous attackers—black Africans—and is prepared to forgive them. What an admirable example of how, with the right attitude, there can be peace and prosperity for all in the new, democratic South Africa.

In December, 2015, an interesting snippet appeared in my daily paper—one that has a reputation for unbiased reporting. It relates to a South African tribal king who was jailed in 2009 for various crimes, and had just lost his latest appeal against the sentence. The writer suggested that this case "highlighted tension between state sovereignty and traditional authority structure." This was a significant observation, as we often wondered if Western style democracy could operate comfortably in a society that had developed under autocratic tribal chiefs such as Shaka Zulu, who has already been mentioned in this narrative.

Comments have been received from various sources, expressing dissatisfaction with the current Head of State. On 18th December, 2015, my newspaper cited just one example. It stated that thousands of middle-class South Africans had marched in Johannesburg, Pretoria and Cape Town as part of a "ZumaMustFall" campaign. In addition to dismissing a finance minister who dared to disagree with him, Zuma had faced allegations of taxpayer-funded upgrades to his private estate, corruption, and even rape. Members of his own party were complaining, and the article continued by mentioning general unhappiness with "the lack of change in the country more than 20 years after the end of apartheid." A spokesman was quoted as saying, "This is not what Mandela spent 27 years in jail for."

In July, 2016, two of our ex neighbors sent us their perspectives on the current situation. The first confirmed that problems are caused by people being elevated to senior positions with little or no experience, and that jobs are being given to "previously disadvantaged" people. As a result, standards of service delivery have fallen, and corruption is a very big problem. Government departments no longer employ or recruit white males. Many promises were made to improve black communities, but these have not been forthcoming. There are many squatter camps, and poor housing areas without running water.

For the ordinary white folk, we are told that life goes on much the same, but you have to learn how to cope with the poor quality of service. Yes, all schools are now integrated, and about 90 percent of pupils are black. This has led to the creation of many private schools which, although multi-ethnic, have lower class sizes and higher educational standards than have the state schools. Whilst the wealth gap between races remains, there is a growing number of very rich black people.

Our second neighbor confirmed the presence of both wealthy and middle-class indigenous Africans, but added that the vast majority remain extremely poor—perhaps even more so than before majority rule. The unemployment situation is drastic, and crime has increased. Many people are seen scratching through rubbish bags and waste dumps to find something of value. The situation has been made worse by the influx of many migrants from the Congo, Nigeria, and other African countries. The poor blacks are often treated very badly by their peers if they go to government offices or clinics for help, and there is evidence of a "bribe" culture if a person wants to get things done. This very jaundiced view concludes with the statement that many blacks would rather go back to the apartheid era, as they were treated better then.

When one of our friends was asked about developments since the first democratic elections, the response was an internet link to an on-line article entitled: "The antithesis of apartheid". It was written in November, 2015, and concerns an all-Afrikaner settlement called "Orania", which has been developed on land privately purchased in the year 1991. From small beginnings, it is now a township covering about 30 square miles, and housing over 1,000 people. Afrikaans is the sole language used and all work, whether skilled or menial, is done by white people. The report states that it is a very safe, happy, self-sufficient community, with all the modern social and environmental services. The schools have a 100 percent success rate in the state matriculation examinations, and send pupils to universities all over South Africa.

Surely a successful enterprise like this, which obeys all the rules, troubles nobody, but just wishes to retain its traditional lifestyle, is to be applauded. But then, what if English-speaking whites followed the example and started their own township? Maybe the Zulus could do the same, and then the Xhosas, the Sothos, the Tswanas, the Ndebeles, and so on. Imagine each of these groups living peacefully, troubling nobody, and preserving their own race, language, and culture.

Would this be a Utopia to be admired? But oh dear, the wheel would have turned a full circle—we would be back to just what apartheid was designed for: separate development!

So what can the future hold for South Africa? Enforced separate development may have ended, but severe differences between the haves and the have-nots remain. Twenty or 30 years is nevertheless a short time in the history of any country. New leaders will be appointed; new heroes will emerge. Perhaps new generations are needed, who would have no experience of the old ways, but have the talent and desire to see their nation grow and prosper. We can only hope that, maybe 50 or 100 years from now, historians will be able to look back at South Africa's apartheid era and its aftermath, and conclude that it was just a part of the growing pains of what had by then become a peaceful, successful, and united nation to be envied and emulated the world over.

Afterword

Was It Worth It?

LIFE WHILST WE WERE in South Africa may have had its problems, but it has not always been easy trying to re-establish ourselves back in the UK. We were not like students returning from a gap year or two; we were well into middle-age, with adult children, and no job.

On a financial note, when we emigrated in 1975, the foreign exchange rate was 1.78 SA rands to a GB pound. When we returned 20 years later, it was 5.77 rands to the pound. Thus, we certainly did not come back rich, and had to start building our lives again, if not exactly from the bottom, then certainly from less than half way up. To make matters worse, I paid into a South African pension scheme for much of our time there. What I received back in 2005 was converted at the rate of 11.10 rands to the pound and, in 2016, this worsened to 22.19 to the pound. Ah well, who needs money anyway (sob!).

During our time in South Africa I had lost my job three times, had been taken hostage, had my car and other possessions stolen, and had been in at least one situation that might have led to life-threatening violence. Had we stayed in the UK, and assuming regular employment, we would have paid off our mortgage many years before retirement, built up a decent bank balance, and been able to enjoy some of the luxuries of life. So, looking back, was the 20 years overseas a rather foolhardy exercise, was it really worth it?

You bet it was worth it! The answer is a definite, unequivocal, resounding "Yes." How else could we have met so many interesting people, seen so many wonderful sights, done so many interesting things. This was a life experience that could not be acquired through expensive holidays, but only by living there and absorbing ourselves in the local culture.

We have so many good memories of our time in South Africa, and are still in contact with some of the friends there. As reminders, we have our photographs, tape recordings, videos, and souvenirs. Another question that we are often asked is: "Do we want to go back to that country?" The answer to this one is an equally resounding "No". This was a chapter of our lives that has now ended, and we probably overstayed our welcome by several years.

Before I add my own final thoughts and conclusions, each family member has been invited to briefly share theirs, starting with my wife.

> Susan writes: Twenty years in South Africa and 21 years since we returned to Blighty. A tall order to try and encapsulate my feelings and thoughts in one short paragraph!
>
> It is the end of July 1995 and the house in Benoni sold and the international removers have been and packed up all our worldly goods to send them across the sea and back to the U.K. Charles is already on his way to stay with a South African school friend who is already in England. Our air tickets are booked via Cairo, so Mike and I have a few days to visit Egypt on our way home. So many good memories, wonderful friends we made while living in Benoni, a beautiful country with some of the best sightseeing in the World. A good place to bring up children in such a near perfect climate. An amazing diversity of different people in the Rainbow Nation that makes up the population of South Africa. Great sadness in having to leave all this behind us. The worst thing was leaving David behind because he wasn't sure that he was ready to return to the U.K. at this time. So a very tearful farewell.
>
> So much to tempt us back to the U.K. though; after all, we never went for good, or did we? We thought

we would give it a try for a couple of years and then go home! Twenty years later, we were still there. Two very elderly mothers to return to, two sisters, one brother, nieces, nephews, cousins, aunts, uncles. Our own flesh and blood, so good to be able to see them all again and to become part of an extended family once more.

Would I do it again? Oh, without a doubt. Do I miss South Africa? Hardly, only the weather! That was then and this is now and there should only ever be *now*!

Peter preferred to be interviewed, rather than try to commit his thoughts to paper. He said that the best thing at first was the environment, especially the wildlife and countryside. Much later, when he was a student, he appreciated the opportunity to become involved in the more radical, anti-establishment counter-culture, which included the emerging non-racial music scene where he played bass guitar in an "alternative" rock band. He still has vivid memories of witnessing clashes between students, peacefully protesting academics, and aggressive police on campus. The belief in a future that was better than the prevailing political reality was a cause worth fighting for, and something to look forward to.

For a year, before going to university, Peter worked as a junior sales representative for the same company as I did. Part of his job was visiting clients with his co-worker, a Zulu man named Moscow Mbambo. Peter remains very grateful that Moscow showed him the "other side" of the apartheid situation, including what life was like in an African township. This opened his eyes to the world beyond white suburbia and segregated education.

Sadly, Peter confessed that the experience as a whole had not been an easy one for him, and it still leaves scars. He was aged nine when we left the UK—old enough to have developed a sense of identity and stability. The educational system he was thrust into was chauvinistic, and not conducive to stimulating original and creative thinking, in contrast to the system he left behind in the UK. He felt a foreigner for most of the time in South Africa, and then a foreigner again when he returned to the UK. Just as he was starting to feel comfortable about being a South African and wanting to remain, at least for a few more years, he had to leave that country to avoid conscription into the armed forces. It was not just the time to be spent in the army that was the problem, but what the conscripts were obliged to do in helping to maintain the oppressive regime (at least according to the stories that filtered back to the general public).

Peter summed up his thoughts by saying that he could have achieved more if he had stayed longer in South Africa, including his musical development. It still leaves him with a feeling of being "unfinished."

David, had not yet reached his seventh birthday when we docked at Cape Town, and he remained in Benoni for nearly two years after the rest of the family had left. He comments:

> It is hard to believe that I have now been back in England almost as long as I lived in South Africa. My time in South Africa feels like a much longer period, probably because it's where I grew up.
>
> I have a feeling of ambivalence when I think back over my 21 years in South Africa. There are many aspects that don't hold fond memories for me, school years being one of them. Many facets of the oppressive Government filtered through to the way schools were run, and I was seldom at ease in the Afrikaner dominated environment. The prospect of being conscripted into the army loomed on the horizon. The two jobs I had were respectively in water pump and lead acid battery manufacturing companies located on a dismal industrial estate in Benoni. Both were overshadowed by particularly unpleasant bosses. So, school and work experiences are perhaps best forgotten.
>
> Whilst growing up, I had aspirations for writing and I remember often feeling there was something in the South African landscape and climate that felt inspirational, and which I would not be able to experience elsewhere. The feeling is partly captured in South African music by artists such as Abdullah Ibrahim, and it's what makes me feel partly South African today.
>
> Despite my experiences (and they weren't all bad), South Africa runs through my veins. I officially have dual

citizenship of South Africa and the U.K. and I genuinely feel that dual citizenship. I have returned to South Africa a couple of times since I left, mostly visiting areas such as Cape Town which I saw little of whilst living there. During the visits I was happy to be reacquainted with the familiar country but, with no friends or family now living there, South Africa no longer holds a pull, and I can't see myself going back there again. I feel lucky to have made a lifelong South African friend who now lives in New Zealand, so perhaps that will be the next destination for me.

Charles' situation was different, in that he was born in South Africa about two years after we arrived there. He then joined us when we returned to the UK, aged 18, having lived in Benoni for his whole life until that point. He summarized his thoughts as follows:

> I miss a country and culture which is focused on the future more than its past. I miss what I see as the more open and less ambiguous demeanor of South Africans, because I believe that I have that mindset myself. South Africa has benefitted from an optimistic can-do American-style mindset, which doesn't feature as prominently in the UK. There's a sense of groundedness that one develops, living on a wild, harsh continent, which contributes to the vitality of African culture. This green and pleasant island of the UK feels different. Then there's the weather and the outdoors of course: holidays on the beautiful Natal coast and trips to game reserves. I was fortunate to have spent a lot of my childhood outdoors.
>
> Not that the UK hasn't offered many things I wouldn't have had staying in South Africa: good educational and job opportunities, the global melting pot of London, access to the rest of Europe, all of which I have taken advantage of. The UK also offered security and sanctuary from the complications of living in a country with a centuries-old legacy of violence, racial division and inequality, none of which was going to be resolved quickly following the end of apartheid. The UK is comparatively dull with its stability and security, but that's a trade-off you'd expect.

I was excited at the prospect of moving to the UK and experiencing all these new things, to see if my impressions and stereotypes of Britain would be matched by first-hand experience. But being suddenly uprooted from my hometown, which was all I'd known until leaving for the UK, has weighed on my mind in the time since, and I feel some envy towards friends who return to their hometown regularly.

In 2015 I visited South Africa, including Benoni, for the first time since leaving. Walking around my old neighborhood, seeing my old school and other familiar sights, was a great experience, though bittersweet, as I knew virtually no-one in my hometown. If I'd had more time I'd have visited our old next door neighbors who still live the same house—nice to know that some things have remained the same.

The country I saw for the first time in 20 years had much improved infrastructure, in particular public transport. Violent crime is half the rate it was, but is still very high by European standards. One major problem still to be resolved is electrical black-outs, as the government has not expanded the energy supply at the rate the economy has grown. In summary, I'd say South Africa has been a "two steps forward, one step back country" over the last 20 years. In this regard, it is in line with other large developing nations. However, it still faces many on-going struggles, although the direction of travel is positive.

It was a tad surprising for me to learn of the regrets that our three sons still have, and it sends a message to those who may also be contemplating emigration. It is obviously not just a simple case of adventure and the excitement of new experiences, coupled perhaps with a better climate and quality of life. It is being aware of possible threats, especially to young people in their formative years, to self-identity, a sense of belonging, and the place that a person can call home.

If asked what the very top highlights were for me personally, it would be a very difficult question to answer. It all revolves around the mind-broadening experience of living in a different environment, with customs, practices and attitudes that were in contrast to those with which we were familiar in the country of our birth. Such exposure helps to avoid parochialism, improves understanding of what life is all about, hopefully helps generate tolerance for things that are different, and ultimately enhances the development of wisdom.

Of course, some of the gems of our stay have been mentioned throughout this book. The "wow" factors included sights such as Table Mountain, the Blyde River Canyon, elephants crossing the road in front of us, and the very moving African singing. Often it is people that generate the most enduring memories. Here is one final anecdote. South Africa had been isolated for a long time, suffering economic sanctions and being banned from international sporting competitions. Following the first democratic elections, the nation craved for the chance to re-enter the international arena. As has already been stated, rugby was the national sport, and was dominated by the Afrikaans sector.

When the country was given the privilege of hosting the 1995 rugby world cup, the reaction there was one of unbridled euphoria. There was just one slight concern. As this was mostly an Afrikaners' sport, would there be any support from the other races and, in particular, the black government? South Africa reached the final, to be played against the New Zealand team on 25th April. The fact that Nelson Mandela arrived to wish the team well, and he was wearing a rugby shirt, was a magnanimous gesture that united the whole nation behind the team.

My understanding of this sport is minimal, but it was a hard-fought game that was tied at full-time. Thus there was a period of extra time. As the game continued, it seemed as if another factor was at work. We may be in the realms of fantasy here, but it was if some force emanating from the whole nation was united, and was enabling the home team members to play at a level over and above their normal ability. South Africa was the victor, and the country went ballistic as soon as the final whistle was blown. Motor cars drove around with their horns blowing, barbeques were lit in the streets, and strangers stopped to shake your hand.

This was a pivotal moment for the country. After all those years of hardship and uncertainty, heading into the unknown of a democracy to which South Africa had not experienced before, something good had happened. Was this a sign that everything would turn out well, that there would be peace and prosperity for everyone? Unfortunately, the recent news reports indicate that the "Rainbow Nation" envisaged by Nelson Mandela is yet to be. We can only hope for a better future for all in that outstanding country.

www.ingramcontent.com/pod-product-compliance
Lightning Source LLC
Chambersburg PA
CBHW070914160426
43193CB00011B/1456